1 Introduction

The underlying shocks that precipitated the financial crisis of 2007-2009 quickly spread across global financial markets and were amplified at an unprecedented scale. The strikingly global nature of the crisis has revived interest in the international coordination of financial regulation. Regulatory reforms and the strengthening of coordination between national financial regulators are prominent items on the international reform agenda. The Financial Stability Board (FSB) was set up by the G-20 countries during the crisis to create guidelines for regulatory coordination and the supervision of systemic risk in the international financial system.[1]

This paper, using a game-theoretic model, analyzes the incentives of national regulators towards international cooperation when there is systemic risk in global financial markets. In the model, systemic risk in financial markets is generated through asset fire sales. The model shows that in the absence of cooperation, independent regulators choose inefficiently low regulatory standards compared to regulation levels that would be chosen by a central regulator. A central regulator internalizes systemic risk and improves welfare in cooperating countries. The model also demonstrates that common central regulation will voluntarily emerge only between sufficiently similar countries.

Key features of a third generation of bank regulation principles, popularly known as Basel III, strengthen capital regulations and add new elements to Basel bank regulation principles such as liquidity and leverage ratio requirements. With Basel III, the objective of regulation aimed at creating a level playing field for internationally active banks is supported by an objective of creating sound regulatory practices that will contain systemic risk in national and international financial markets, and prevent pro-cyclical amplification of these risks over time. In this paper, I revisit the issue of coordinating international financial regulation in light of recent developments in the international regulatory infrastructure.

Acharya (2003, 2009) and Dell'Ariccia and Marquez (2006) are notable studies in the literature on international financial regulation. All three of these studies focus on the level playing field objective of financial regulation and examine the benefits to international coordination of financial regulation under externalities that operate through the competition in loan markets. This paper diverges from the previous literature by focusing on systemic externalities across financial markets generated by fire sales of assets. I examine the effects of systemic externalities on the nature of international financial regulation in the absence of cooperation between regulators, as well as its effects on the incentives of national regulators towards cooperation. The paper also contributes to the literature by examining the effects of structural differences across countries on the choice of regulatory standards when countries are linked through systemic externalities in international

---

[1] The Financial Stability Board (FSB) was established after the 2009 G-20 London summit in April 2009; it is the successor to the Financial Stability Forum (FSF). The FSF was founded in 1999 by the G-7 finance ministers and central bank governors.

financial markets. I show herein that common central regulation voluntarily emerges only between sufficiently similar countries.

During times of distress, asset prices can move away from the fundamental values and assets can be traded at fire sale prices. When firms or financial intermediaries face liquidity shocks, and debt-overhang, collateral or commitment problems prevent them from borrowing or issuing new equity they may have to sell assets to generate the required resources. If the shocks are wide spread throughout an industry or an economy, then potentially deep-pocket outsiders will emerge as the buyers of the assets. However, some assets are industry-specific: when they are redeployed by outsiders, they will be less productive, and they will be sold to outsiders at a discount. This idea, which originated in Williamson (1988) and Shleifer and Vishny (1992), was later employed by fire sales models such as Lorenzoni (2008), Gai et al. (2008), Acharya et al. (2010) and Korinek (2011).

Industry-specific assets can be physical, or they can be portfolios of financial intermediaries because many of these contain exotic tailor-made financial assets (Gai et al., 2008). The asset specificity idea is captured in this paper through a decreasing returns to scale technology for outsiders, similar to the ones proposed by Kiyotaki and Moore (1997), Lorenzoni (2008), Gai et al. (2008), and Korinek (2011). The less efficient technology of outsiders makes the situation even worse for distressed intermediaries because they have to accept higher discounts to sell more assets. Empirical and anecdotal evidence suggests the existence of fire sales of physical as well as financial assets.[2]

These facts indicate that when numerous intermediaries concurrently face the same types of shocks and sell assets simultaneously, asset prices can fall, which forces the intermediaries to sell additional assets. Because an individual intermediary takes the market price as given and decides how much of its assets to sell to continue operating at an optimal scale, each intermediary ignores the negative externality of its asset sales on others. In a financially integrated world, intermediaries from different countries sell assets in a global market to potentially the same set of buyers. Therefore, initial shocks that hit individual countries can be amplified in globally integrated financial markets.

I consider this systemic externality in this paper, and also seek answers to the following questions: How do national regulators behave under this systemic externality if the regulators act non-cooperatively? Would an individual regulator tighten or relax regulation when regulation is tightened in another country? Would national regulators relinquish their authority to a central international regulator who would impose the same set of regulatory standards across countries?

---

[2] Using a large sample of commercial aircraft transactions, Pulvino (2002) shows that distressed airlines sell aircraft at a 14% discount from the average market price. This discount exists when the airline industry is depressed but not when it is booming. Coval and Stafford (2007) show that fire sales occur in equity markets when mutual funds engage in sales of similar stocks. fire sales have been shown to exist in international settings as well; for examples, surges in foreign direct investment into emerging markets have been recorded during Asian and Latin American financial crises. In particular, Krugman (2000), Aguiar and Gopinath (2005), and Acharya et al. (2010) show that asset sales to outsiders during these crises were associated with high discounts, and that many foreigners flipped the assets they purchased to domestics once the crises abated at very high returns.

How do asymmetries across countries affect the nature of regulatory standards and the incentives of national regulators towards international cooperation?

Briefly, I propose a three-period, two-good model that features two countries with independent regulators. In each country there is a continuum of banks. Banks are protected by limited liability, and there is deposit insurance. Banks borrow consumption goods from local deposit markets, and invest in a productive asset in the first period.

All uncertainty in the model is resolved at the beginning of the second period and one of the two states of the world is realized: a good or a bad state. In the good state there are no shocks and banks' investments produce net positive returns in the last period. However, in the bad state, banks' investments are distressed and they have to be restructured to produce the normal positive returns that are obtained in good times.

A continuum of global investors with large resources in the second period can purchase productive assets in the second period to produce consumption goods in the third and final period. Assets in different countries are perfect substitutes for global investors. However, global investors are not as productive as the domestic banks in managing domestic assets and face decreasing returns to scale from these assets.

I solve the equilibrium of this model by backwards induction. Following the shocks in the interim period, banks need to sell some fraction of their assets in a global capital market to pay for the restructuring costs. An asset sale in the bad state is unavoidable because other domestic resources required to carry out the restructuring process are unavailable. The price of the productive asset is determined in a competitive market in which banks from the two countries and global investors meet.

I show that a higher initial investment by banks in either of these countries will lead to a lower price for the productive asset in this market. If the asset price falls below a minimum threshold, return to the assets that can be retained by the banks is lower than the value of the initial investment, and the banks become insolvent. I call this case a systemic failure. Depositors encounter real losses when a systemic failure occurs because returns to the remaining bank assets do not cover depositors' initial investment.

Regulation in this model can be interpreted as a minimum capital ratio requirement. Each regulator determines the initial regulatory standard by taking into account the equilibrium in the asset market in the interim period. Due to the systemic externality discussed above, banks always leverage up to the maximum by borrowing funds from the local deposit market. In other words, the minimum capital ratio always binds. Therefore, the initial investment level of banks in a given country is determined completely by the regulatory standard.

In the first period, regulators act simultaneously and choose the regulatory standard for their domestic banks by taking the regulatory standard in the other country as given. I show that when the countries are symmetric, there exists a unique symmetric Nash equilibrium of the game between the two regulators. Moreover, regulation levels in the two countries are strategic substitutes: if one regulator tightens the regulatory standard in its jurisdiction, the other regulator optimally loosens its regulatory standard. The intuition behind this result is as follows: When the first country reduces the maximum leverage level (i.e., tightens regulatory standards), the extent of the fire sale of assets in the bad state by banks in that country are reduced, and a higher price is realized for the assets sold by these banks. This increases the expected returns in the bad state, which allows the regulator in the other country to relax regulation levels.

I show that, due to this systemic risk, regulatory standards in equilibrium when regulators act non-cooperatively will be inefficiently lax compared to regulatory standards that would be chosen by a central regulator. A central regulator aims to maximize the total welfare of the two countries, and internalizes these externalities. I assume that, for political reasons, the central regulator has to choose the same regulation levels in both countries. If the two countries are symmetric, I show that forming a regulatory union will increase welfare in both. Therefore, it is incentive compatible for the independent regulators of symmetric countries to relinquish their authority to a central regulator.

I also consider the incentives of regulators when there are asymmetries between countries, with a focus on the asymmetries in the asset returns. In particular, I assume that banks in one country are uniformly more productive than the banks in the other country in terms of managing the long-term asset. I also show that cooperation would voluntarily emerge only between sufficiently similar countries. In particular, the regulator in the high-return country chooses lower regulatory standards in equilibrium and is less willing to compromise on stricter regulatory standards.

Interest in the international coordination of financial regulation is not an entirely recent phenomenon. Arguments in favor of coordination and harmonization of regulatory policies across countries were made in the 1988 Basel Accord (Basel I) which focused on credit risk and set minimum capital requirements for internationally active banks and was enforced in the G-10 countries in 1992.[3]

However, Basel I did not create an entirely level playing field for internationally active banks because countries retained a significant degree of discretion about different dimensions of regulation. Furthermore, rapid developments in financial markets, especially more complex financial products brought about by financial innovation, created significant differences about the stringency of capital regulations across countries in practice (Barth et al., 2008). These developments created a challenge for regulators and paved the way for Basel II.[4]

While progress on the implementation of Basel II was slower than expected, the global financial

---

[3]The intent of Basel I was to strengthen the soundness and stability of the international banking system and to diminish competitive inequality among international banks by creating a level playing field Basel (1988).

[4]Basel I was updated in 2004 with more sophisticated sets of rules and principles for capital regulation that were intended to accommodate the developments in global financial markets. A 2006 survey by the Bank for International Settlements (BIS) showed that 95 countries (comprising 13 BSBC member countries plus 82 non-BSBC jurisdictions) had planned to implement Basel II by 2015.

crisis renewed urgency about increased cooperation and the better regulation of international financial markets, in part because insufficient policy coordination between countries and deficiencies in Basel II regulatory mechanisms were blamed for the severe contagion of the crisis. Most of the international regulatory mechanisms proposed prior to the crisis had emphasized the soundness of financial institutions individually (micro-prudential regulation), but had neglected regulatory standards that could enhance the stability of the financial system as a whole by considering systemic risks (macro-prudential regulation). The model in this paper focuses on macro-prudential regulation in the context of regulating systemic risk in the international banking system.

The paper proceeds as follows. Section 2 contains a brief summary of related literature. Section 3 provides the basics of the model and presents the main results of the paper without resorting to a particular functional form. International financial regulation between asymmetric countries is considered in Section 4. Section 5 investigates the robustness of the results obtained from the basic model to some changes in the model environment. Section 6 shows the set of parameter ranges for which systemic failures occur in the uncoordinated equilibrium when countries are symmetric. Conclusions are presented in Section 7. All proofs are provided in the Appendix.

2 Literature Review

This paper belongs to the international financial regulation theory that has developed in recent decades. This paper is closest to Acharya (2003), Dell'Ariccia and Marquez (2006), Acharya (2009), and Bengui (2011). In particular, Dell'Ariccia and Marquez (2006) investigate the incentives of national regulators to form a regulatory union in a two-country banking model, where a single bank from each country competes for loans in both markets in a Bertrand differentiated products setup. If one of the banks is allowed to expand its balance sheet, low average returns to bank loans will be realized in both markets. Banks in this model are also endowed with a costly monitoring technology. Low average returns reduce incentives of banks to monitor, and hence undermines their stability. The authors show that, under this externality, independent national regulators will implement lower capital requirements compared to capital requirements that would be implemented by a central regulator. They also show that symmetric countries always gain from cooperation, whereas a cooperation emerges voluntarily only between sufficiently similar asymmetric countries. The coordination problem for asymmetric countries as presented in this paper is similar to Dell'Ariccia and Marquez (2006). However, in that model the asymmetry between countries was due to differences in regulators' exogenously specified tastes and preferences. In this paper I consider asymmetries that are due to structural differences across countries, such as differences in asset returns.

Acharya (2003) shows that convergence in international capital adequacy standards cannot be effective unless it is accompanied by convergence in other aspects of banking regulation, such as closure policies. Externalities in his model are in the form of cost of investment in the risky asset. He assumes that a bank in one country increases costs of investment for itself and for a bank in the other country as it invest more in the risky asset and thereby creates externalities for the bank in the neighboring country.

In the model considered by Acharya (2009), failure of a bank creates both negative and positive externalities for surviving banks. Negative externality is the increase in the cost of the deposits for surviving banks through a reduction in overall available funds. Positive externalities are strategic benefits that arise either through depositor migration from the failing banks to surviving banks, or through acquisition of the failed banks' assets and businesses by surviving banks. He shows that that if the negative externality dominates positive externalities, banks in different regions will choose their investments to be highly correlated compared to globally optimal correlation levels. Acharya calls this fact "systemic risk shifting".

This paper also differs from previously mentioned studies in terms of its source for the externalities between national financial markets. I focus on externalities between national financial markets that operate through asset markets and asset prices whereas the studies cited above considered externalities that operate through costs in the loan or deposit markets. In this paper, systemic risk in international financial markets arises as banks from two countries experience correlated liquidity shocks, and financial amplification effects are triggered due to fire sales. In that regard, this paper is closest to Bengui (2011), but mainly differs from Bengui (2011) by considering the coordination problem under systemic risk for structurally different countries. On the other hand, Bengui (2011) considers the coordination problem for symmetric countries with risk averse individuals and imperfectly correlated shocks across countries. As this paper affirms, provision of macro-prudential regulation is insufficient when countries act independently, and regulatory standards are strategic substitutes across countries. He also shows that risk taking could be higher in nationally regulated economies compared to the competitive equilibrium, and that starting from a competitive equilibrium unilateral introduction of a (small) regulation could be welfare reducing for the country introducing the regulation.

Another branch of this literature considers regulation of a multi-national bank that operates across two countries. Two notable studies, Dalen and Olsen (2003) and Holthausen and Rønde (2004), focus on the tension between home and host country regulation of a multi-national bank where informational asymmetries are the driving force of regulatory competition. Unlike these studies, my paper focuses on a model in which banks invest in a single country and are therefore regulated only by their home country, but interact with each other in global asset markets. The tension between regulators in my model arises from the externalities that banks in different countries create for each other in global asset markets during times of distress.

This study can also be viewed as a part of the broader literature on macroeconomic policy coordination that was especially active especially from late 1970s through the 1990s. Cooper (1985) and Persson and Tabellini (1995) provide extensive reviews of this literature. Hamada (1974, 1976) are the pioneer studies in the application of the game-theoretic approach to strategic interactions among national governments.

Last, this paper is also related to the literature that features asset fire sales. The common theme across these studies is that, under certain conditions, asset prices can move away from the fundamental values and assets can be traded in markets at fire sale prices. One reason for fire sales is the combined effect of asset-specificity and correlated shocks that hit an entire industry or economy. Origins of this idea can be found in Williamson (1988) and Shleifer and Vishny (1992) which claim that fire sales are more likely when major players in an industry face correlated shocks and the assets of the indusry are not easily redeployable in other industries. In such a scenario, a firm needs to sell assets to restructure and continue operations at a smaller scale; however, it cannot sell its assets at full value because other firms in the same industry are experiencing similar problems. Outside investors would buy and manage these assets but they are not as sophisticated as the firms in the industry. Therefore, they would be willing to pay less than the full value of the assets to the distressed firms. Moreover, unsophisticated investors may face decreasing returns in the amounts of assets they employ. This possibility makes the situation even worse for distressed firms because if many of them try to sell assets to outside investors simultaneously, they will have to accept higher discounts.

The closest papers in this literature to mine are Lorenzoni (2008), Gai et al. (2008) and Korinek (2011) which essentially address the same question: how do privately optimal borrowing and investment levels of financial intermediaries compare to the socially optimal levels under pecuniary externalities in financial markets generated through asset fire sales? In these studies, the reasons for fire sales are limited commitment on financial contracts and the fact that asset prices are determined in a spot market. Lorenzoni (2008) and Gai et al. (2008) consider a single-country, three-period model with a continuum of banks. Banks borrow from consumers and offer them state-contingent contracts. In the interim period, banks are hit by shocks and need to sell assets in some states to restructure distressed investments. These papers show that there exists over-borrowing and hence over-investment in risky assets in a competitive setting compared to the socially optimal solution. Because in the competitive setting each bank treats the market price of assets as given when it makes borrowing and investment decisions in the initial period, it does not internalize the externalities created for other banks through fire sales. The planner considers the fact that a higher investment will translate into lower prices for capital sold by banks during the times of distress. The main difference between my paper and these papers is that they focus on issues in single-country cases to the exclusion of issues related to the international dimension of regulation.

Asset specificity is not the only reason for fire sales. In Allen and Gale (1994, 1998) and Acharya and Yorulmazer (2008) the reason for fire sales is the limited available amount of cash in the market to buy long-term assets offered for sale by agents who need liquid resources immediately. The scarcity of liquid resources leads to necessary discounts in asset prices, a phenomenon known as "cash-in-the-market pricing".

3 Model

This model contains three periods, $t = 0, 1, 2$; and two countries, $i = A, B$. In each country there is a continuum of banks and a continuum of consumers each with a unit mass and a financial regulator. There is also a unit mass of global investors. All agents are risk-neutral.

There are two goods in this economy: a consumption good and a capital good (i.e., the liquid and illiquid assets). Consumers are endowed with e units of consumption goods at $t = 0$, and none at later periods.[5]

Banks have a technology that converts consumption goods into capital goods one-to-one at $t = 0$. Capital goods that are managed by a bank until the last period yield $R > 1$ consumption goods per unit. Consumption goods are perishable, and the capital fully depreciates at $t = 2$. Capital goods can never be converted into consumption goods.[6]

Banks in each country $i = A, B$ choose the level of investment, n_i, in the capital good at $t = 0$, and borrow the necessary funds from domestic consumers. I consider deposit contracts that are in the form of simple debt contracts, and assume that there is a deposit insurance fund operated by the regulator in each country. Therefore, banks can raise deposits from consumers at a constant and zero net interest rate. I also assume that banks are protected by limited liability.[7]

All uncertainty is resolved at the beginning of $t = 1$: a country lands in good times with probability q, and in bad times with probability $1 - q$. In order to simplify the analysis, I assume that the states of the world at $t = 1$ are perfectly correlated across countries. In good times no banks are hit with shocks, therefore no further actions are taken. Banks keep managing their capital goods and realize the full returns from their investment, Rn_i, in the last period. They make the promised payment, n_i, to consumers, and hence earn a net profit of $(R - 1)n_i$. However, in bad times, the investments of all banks in both countries are distressed. In case of distress, the investment has to be restructured in order to remain productive. Restructuring costs are equal to $c \leq 1$ units of consumption goods per unit of capital. If c is not paid, capital is scrapped (i.e., it fully depreciates).

There are no available domestic resources (i.e., consumption goods) with which to carry out the restructuring of distressed investment at $t = 1$. Only global investors are endowed with liquid resources at this point. Due to a commitment problem, banks cannot borrow the required resources

---

[5] I assume that the initial endowment of consumers is sufficiently large, and it is not a binding constraint in equilibrium.

[6] I focus on a simple, tractable model where there is no safe asset and the liquidity shock at the interim period has a degenerate distribution. I conjecture that relaxing the assumption of no safe asset will not change the qualitative results of this model. If we allow banks to hoard safe assets, and consider a more general distribution of liquidity shocks, banks will hold some optimum amount of safe assets at the initial period for precautionary reasons. These precautionary savings, however, will not be sufficient to cover liquidity needs under large realizations of shocks. In these states of the world, asset fire sales will be unavoidable, and that inevitability will generate the externality between countries that is the crucial part of the current model.

[7] Limited liability and deposit insurance assumptions are imposed to match reality and to simplify the analysis of the model. All qualitative results carry on when these assumptions are removed, as shown is Section 6.

from global investors. My particular assumption is that individual banks cannot commit to pay their production to global investors in the last period.[8] The only way for banks to raise necessary funds for restructuring is to sell some fraction of the investment to global investors in an exchange of consumption goods.

These capital sales by banks will carry the features of a fire sale: the capital good will be traded below its fundamental value for banks, and the price will decrease as banks try to sell more capital. Banks in each country will retain only a fraction of their assets after fire sales. If the asset price falls below a threshold, the expected return on the assets that can be retained by banks will be lower than the value of the initial investment; hence, banks will become insolvent.[9] I call this situation a "systemic failure".

Figure 1: Timing of the Model

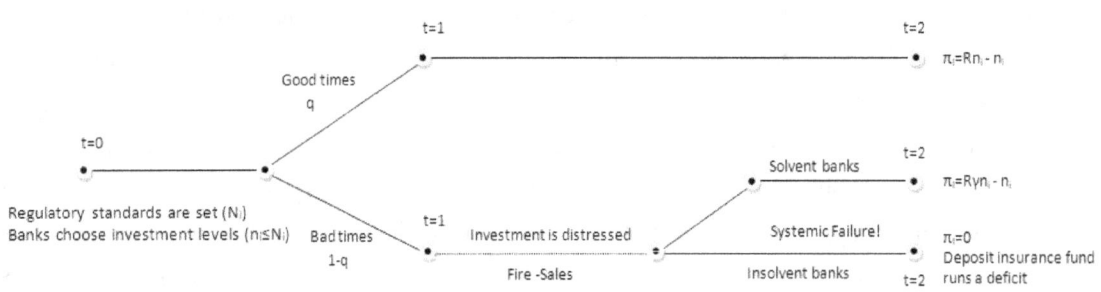

Once it is known that banks are insolvent, deposit insurance requires the bank owners to manage their capital goods to realize the returns in the last period. The regulator then seizes banks' returns, and makes the promised payments to depositors. The deposit insurance fund runs a deficit. If fire sales are sufficiently mild, however, then banks will have enough assets to make the promised payments to the depositors. In this case banks remain solvent, but compared to good times they make smaller profits. This sequence of events is illustrated in Figure 1.

Banks are subject to regulation in the form of an upper limit on initial investment levels.[10] Regulatory standards are set, independently, by the individual national regulators at the beginning of $t = 0$. The regulator of country i determines the maximum investment allowed for banks in its jurisdiction, N_i, while taking into account the regulation in the other country, N_j, as given.

---

[8]For simplicity, I assume that the commitment problem is extreme (i.e., banks cannot commit to pay any fraction of their production to global investors). Assuming a milder but sufficiently strong commitment problem where banks can commit a small fraction of their production, as in Lorenzoni (2008) and Gai et al. (2008), does not change the qualitative results of this paper.

[9]Because all uncertainty is resolved at the beginning of $t = 1$, the expected return to capital retained by banks after fire sales, which is certain at that point, is R units of consumption goods per unit of capital.

[10]This regulation becomes equivalent to a minimum capital ratio requirement when we introduce a costly bank equity capital to the model, as shown in Section 5. I abstract from costly equity capital in the basic model in order to simplify the exposition.

Investment levels of banks in country i have to satisfy $n_i \leq N_i$ at $t = 0$. The regulatory standard in a country is chosen to maximize the net expected returns on risky investments.

3.1 Global Investors

Global investors are endowed with unlimited resources of consumption goods at $t = 1$.[11] They can purchase capital, y, from banks in each country at $t = 1$ and employ this capital to produce $F(y)$ units of consumption goods at $t = 2$. For global investors capital supplied by the banks in these two countries are identical.[12] Let P denote the market price of the capital good at $t = 1$.[13] Because we have a continuum of global investors, each investor treats the market price as given, and chooses the amount of capital to purchase, y, to maximize net returns from investment at $t = 2$.

$$\max_{y \geq 0} F(y) - Py \tag{1}$$

The amount of assets they optimally buy satisfies the following first order conditions

$$F'(y) = P \tag{2}$$

The first order condition above determines global investors' (inverse) demand function for the capital good. Using this, we can define their demand function $D(P)$ as follows:

$$y = F'(P)^{-1} \equiv D(P) \tag{3}$$

We need to impose some structure on the return function of global investors and the model parameters in order to ensure that the equilibrium of this model is well-behaved.

3.2 Basic Assumptions

Assumption 1 (CONCAVITY).

$$F'(y) > 0 \text{ and } F''(y) < 0 \text{ for all } y \geq 0, \text{ with } F'(0) \leq R.$$

---

[11] The assumption that there are some global investors with unlimited resources at the interim period when no one else has resources can be justified with reference to the empirical facts during the Asian and Latin American financial crises. Krugman (2000), Aguiar and Gopinath (2005), and Acharya et al. (2010) provide evidence that, when those countries were hit by shocks and their assets were distressed, some outside investors with large liquid resources bought their assets.

[12] The assumption that capital goods in the two countries are perfect substitutes for global investors is for simplicity. The externality that is central to this model is due to the fact that supply conditions in one country affect the prices that the banks in the other country can obtain for their assets in distress times. A milder assumption of imperfect substitutes would generate the same externality at a cost of higher complexity.

[13] Price of capital at $t = 0$ will be one as long as there is positive investment, and the price of capital at $t = 2$ will be zero because capital fully depreciates at this point.

Assumption $CONCAVITY$ says that although global investors' return is strictly increasing the amount of capital employed ($F'(y) > 0$), they face decreasing returns to scale in the production of consumption goods ($F''(y) < 0$), as opposed to banks that are endowed with a constant returns to scale technology as described above. $F'(0) \leq R$ implies that global investors are less productive than banks at each level of capital employed.

Concavity of the return function implies that the demand function of global investors for capital goods is downward sloping (see Figure 2). Global investors will require higher discounts to absorb more capital from distressed banks at $t = 1$. This assumption intends to capture that distress selling of assets is associated with reduced prices. Using a large sample of commercial aircraft transactions Pulvino (2002) shows that distressed airlines sell aircraft at a 14% discount from the average market price. This discount exists when the airline industry is depressed but not when it is booming. Coval and Stafford (2007) show that fire sales exist in equity markets when mutual funds engage in sales of similar stocks. Furthermore, Krugman (2000), Aguiar and Gopinath (2005), and Acharya et al. (2010) provide significant empirical and anecdotal evidence that during Asian and Latin American crises, foreign acquisitions of troubled countries' assets were very widely spread across industries and assets were sold at sharp discounts. These evidence suggests that foreign investors took control of domestic enterprises mainly because they had liquid resources whereas the locals did not, even though the locals had superior technology and know-how to run the domestic enterprises. Further support for this argument comes from the evidence in Acharya et al. (2010) that many foreigners eventually flipped the assets they acquired during the Asian crisis to locals, and usually made enormous profits from such trades.

The idea that some assets are industry-specific, and hence less productive in the hands of outsiders, has its origins in Williamson (1988) and Shleifer and Vishny (1992). Examples of industry-specific assets include oil rigs and refineries, aircraft, copper mines, pharmaceutical patents, and steel plants. These studies have claimed that when major players in such industries face correlated liquidity shocks and cannot raise external finance due to debt overhang, agency, or commitment problems, they may have to sell assets to outsiders. Outsiders are willing to pay less than the value in best use for the assets of distressed enterprises because they do not have the specific know-how to manage these assets well and therefore face agency costs of hiring specialists to run these assets. The decreasing returns to scale technology assumption captures the inefficiency of outsiders, similar to Kiyotaki and Moore (1997), Lorenzoni (2008), Gai et al. (2008), and Korinek (2011). It is also a reduced way of modeling that global investors first purchase assets that are easy to manage, but as they purchase more assets they will need to buy ones that require sophisticated management and operation skills.

Assumption 2 (ELASTICITY).

$$\epsilon_{P,y} = -\frac{\partial y}{\partial P}\frac{P}{y} = -\frac{F'(y)}{yF''(y)} > 1 \quad \text{for all } y \geq 0$$

Assumption *ELASTICITY* says that global investors' demand for the capital good is elastic. This assumption implies that the amount spent by global investors on asset purchases, $Py = F'(y)y$, is strictly increasing in y. Therefore we can also write Assumption *ELASTICITY* as

$$F'(y) + yF''(y) > 0$$

If this assumption was violated, multiple levels of asset sales would raise a given amount of liquidity, and multiple equilibria in the asset market at $t = 1$ would be possible. This assumption is imposed by Lorenzoni (2008) and Korinek (2011) in order to rule out multiple equilibria under fire sales.[14]

Assumption 3 (REGULARITY).

$$F'(y)F'''(y) - 2F''(y)^2 \leq 0 \quad \text{for all } y \geq 0$$

Assumption *REGULARITY* holds whenever the demand function of global investors is log-concave, but it is weaker than log-concavity.[15] In order to see this, let $\phi(y) \equiv F'(y)$ denote the (inverse) demand function of global investors. We can rewrite Assumption *REGULARITY* as

$$\phi(y)\phi''(y) - 2\phi'(y)^2 \leq 0.$$

We can show that the demand function is log-concave if and only if $\phi(y)\phi''(y) - \phi'(y)^2 \leq 0$. Log-concavity of demand function is a common assumption used in the Cournot games literature (see Amir (1996)); it ensures the existence and uniqueness of equilibrium in a simple *n-player* Cournot game. Therefore, I call it a "regularity" assumption on $F(\cdot)$. Clearly Assumption *REGULARITY* holds whenever the demand function is log-concave. However, Assumption *REGULARITY* is weaker than log-concavity and may also hold if the demand function is log-convex (i.e., if $\phi(y)\phi''(y) - \phi'(y)^2 \geq 0$).

Assumption *REGULARITY* will ensure that the objective functions of regulators are well-behaved. It will be crucial in showing that the equilibrium of this model exists and it is unique.

Many regular return functions satisfy conditions given by Assumptions *CONCAVITY*, *ELASTICITY* and *REGULARITY*. Here are two examples that satisfy all three of the above assumptions:

Example 1 $F(y) = R\ln(1+y)$

Example 2 $F(y) = \sqrt{y + (1/2R)^2}$

---

[14] Gai et al. (2008) provides the leading example where this assumption is not imposed and multiple equilibria in the asset market is therefore considered.

[15] A function is said to be log-concave if the logarithm of the function is concave.

The following example satisfies Assumption *CONCAVITY*, but not Assumptions *ELASTICITY* and *REGULARITY*.

Example 3 $F(y) = y(R - 2\alpha y)$ where $2\alpha y < R$ for all $y \geq 0$.

Assumption 4 (RANGE).
$$1 + (1-q)c < R \leq 1/q$$

Assumption *RANGE* says that the return on investment for banks must not be too low because if they are, equilibrium investment levels will be zero. Nor they must be too high; if they are, equilibrium investment levels will be infinite. This assumption, while not crucial for the results, allows us to focus on interesting cases in which equilibrium investment levels are neither zero nor infinite.

3.3 Equilibrium with Symmetric Countries

In this section I consider only symmetric countries and solve the model by backwards induction. First, I analyze the equilibrium at the interim period in each state of the world, for a given set of investment levels; then I solve the game between the regulators at $t = 0$. Note that, if good times are realized $t = 0$, no further actions need to be taken by any agent. Therefore, at $t = 1$ we need only to analyze the equilibrium of the model for bad times.

I solve the model without resorting to some particular functional form. The results of this paper hold for any functional form that satisfy Assumptions *CONCAVITY*, *ELASTICITY*, and *REGULARITY*.

3.3.1 Crisis and fire sales

Consider the problem of a bank in country i if bad times are realized at $t = 1$. The bank reaches $t = 1$ with a level of investment equal to n_i which was chosen at the initial period. The investment is distressed and must be restructured using liquid resources. The investment will not produce any returns in the last period if it is not restructured.[16] The bank cannot raise external finance from global investors because it cannot commit to pay them in the last period. Therefore, the only way for the bank to raise the funds necessary for restructuring is to sell some fraction of the investment to global investors and use the proceeds to pay for restructuring costs, whereby it can retain another fraction of the investment.

At the beginning of $t = 1$ in bad times, a bank in country i decides what fraction of capital to restructure (χ_i) and what fraction of restructured capital to sell $(1 - \gamma_i)$ to generate the resources for restructuring. Note that γ_i will then represent the fraction of capital that a bank keeps after fire

---

[16]For example, if the assets are physical, restructuring costs can be maintenance costs or working-capital needs.

sales.[17] Thus the bank takes the price of capital (P) as given, and chooses χ_i and γ_i to maximize total returns from that point on

$$\max_{0 \leq \chi_i, \gamma_i \leq 1} \pi_i = R\gamma_i\chi_i n_i + P(1-\gamma_i)\chi_i n_i - c\chi_i n_i \qquad (4)$$

subject to the budget constraint

$$P(1-\gamma_i)\chi_i n_i - c\chi_i n_i \geq 0. \qquad (5)$$

The first term in (4) is the (certain) total return that will be obtained from the unsold part of the restructured assets, which are $\chi_i n_i$, in the last period. The second term is the revenue raised by selling a fraction $(1-\gamma_i)$ of the restructured assets, which are $\chi_i n_i$, at the given market price P. The last term, $c\chi_i n_i$, gives the total cost of restructuring. Budget constraint (5) says that the revenues raised by selling capital must be greater than or equal to the restructuring costs.

By Assumption $CONCAVITY$, the equilibrium price of capital must satisfy $P \leq F'(0) \leq R$, otherwise global investors will not purchase any capital. Later on, I will show that in equilibrium we must also have $c < P$. For the moment, we will assume that the equilibrium price of assets satisfies

$$c < P \leq R \qquad (6)$$

Now, consider the first order conditions of the maximization problem (4) while ignoring the constraints

$$\frac{\partial \pi_i}{\partial \chi_i} = [R\gamma_i + P(1-\gamma_i) - c]n_i \qquad (7)$$

$$\frac{\partial \pi_i}{\partial \gamma_i} = (R-P)\chi_i n_i \qquad (8)$$

From (8) it is obvious that π_i is increasing in γ_i because $P \leq R$ by (6): when the price of capital goods is lower than the return that banks can generate by keeping them, banks want to retain a maximum amount. Choosing γ_i as high as possible implies that the budget constraint will bind. Hence, from (5) we obtain that the fraction of capital goods retained by banks after fire sales is

$$\gamma_i = 1 - \frac{c}{P} \qquad (9)$$

The fraction banks retain after fire sales (γ_i) is increasing in the price of the capital good (P) and

---

[17]Following Lorenzoni (2008) and Gai et al. (2008), I assume that banks have to restructure an asset before selling it. Basically, this means that bank receive the asset price P from global investors, use a part, c, to restructure the asset, and then deliver the restructured assets to global investors. Therefore banks will sell assets only if P is greater than the restructuring cost, c. We could assume, without qualitatively changing our results, that it is the responsibility of global investors to restructure the assets that they purchase. However, the model is more easily solved using the current story.

Figure 2: Equilibrium in the Capital Goods Market

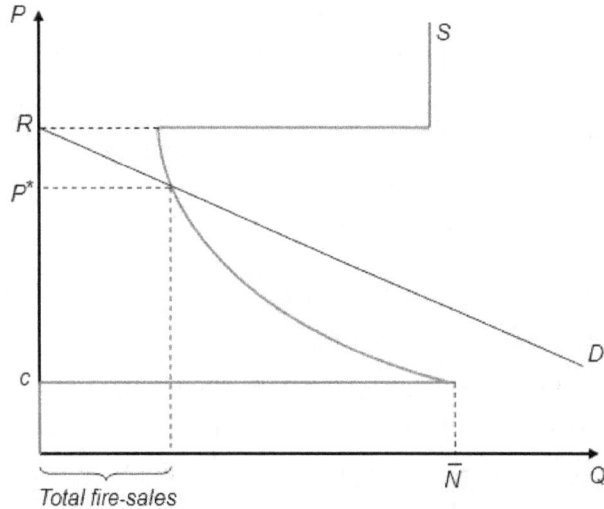

decreasing in the cost of restructuring (c). From (9) we can also obtain the total capital supply of a bank in country i as

$$S_i(P, n_i) = (1 - \gamma_i)n_i = \frac{c}{P}n_i \tag{10}$$

for $c < P \leq R$. This supply curve is downward-sloping and convex, which is standard in the fire sales literature. A negative slope implies that if there is a decrease in the price of assets banks have to sell more assets in order to generate the resources needed for restructuring. This is because banks are selling a valuable investment at a price below the fair value for them due to an exogenous pressure (e.g., paying for restructuring costs).

On the other hand, using (9) we can write the first order condition (7) as

$$\frac{\partial \pi_i}{\partial \chi_i} = R\gamma_i n_i \geq 0 \tag{11}$$

Equation (11) shows that revenues are increasing in χ_i at $t = 1$. Therefore, banks will optimally choose to restructure the full fraction of the investment ($\chi_i = 1$). In other words, scrapping of capital will never arise in equilibrium.

Note that if the capital price is greater than R, banks want to sell all the capital goods they have because they can get at most R per unit by keeping and managing them. If the price is lower than c, however, they will optimally scrap all of their capital ($\chi_i = 0$). As discussed above, prices above R and below c will never arise in equilibrium. The total asset supply curve of banks from the two countries is plotted in Figure 2 for an initial total investment in the two countries of N_0.

3.3.2 Equilibrium in the Capital Market at t=1

Equilibrium price of capital goods, P^*, will be determined by the market clearing condition

$$E(P^*, n_A, n_B) = D(P^*) - S(P^*, n_A, n_B) = 0 \qquad (12)$$

The condition above says that the excess demand in the capital market, denoted by $E(P, n_A, n_B)$, is equal to zero at the equilibrium price. $D(P)$ in Equation (12) is the demand function of global investors which was obtained from the first order conditions of global investors' problem as shown by (3). $S(P, n_A, n_B)$ is the total supply of capital goods. We can obtain it as

$$S(P, n_A, n_B) = \frac{c(n_A + n_B)}{P} \qquad (13)$$

by adding the individual supply of banks in each country given by (10).

This equilibrium is illustrated in Figure 2. Note that the equilibrium price of capital at $t = 1$ will be a function of the initial investment level in the two countries. Therefore, from the perspective of the initial period I denote the equilibrium price as $P^*(n_A, n_B)$.

How does a change in the initial investment level in one of the countries affect the price of capital at $t = 1$? Lemma 1 shows that if investment into the risky asset in one country increases at $t = 0$, a lower price for capital will be realized in the fire sales state at $t = 1$.

Lemma 1. *$P^*(n_i, n_j)$ is decreasing in n_i for $i = A, B$ and $j \neq i$ under Assumptions CONCAVITY and ELASTICITY.*

Proof. See the appendix. □

Lemma 1 implies that higher investment in the risky asset in one country (i.e., a higher n_i) increases the severity of the financial crisis for both countries by lowering the asset prices. This effect is illustrated in Figure 3. Suppose that initial investment level in country A increases, increasing the total investment in the two countries from N_0 to N_1. In this case, banks in country A will have to sell more assets at each price, as can be seen from individual supply function given by (10). Graphically, the total supply curve will shift to the right, as shown by the dotted-line supply curve in Figure 3, which will cause a decrease in the equilibrium price of capital goods. Lower asset prices, by contrast, will induce more fire sales by banks in both countries in the bad state due to the downward-sloping supply curve. This additional result is formalized in Lemma 2.

Lemma 2. *Equilibrium fraction of assets sold in each country, $1 - \gamma^*(n_i, n_j)$, is increasing in n_i for $i = A, B$ under Assumptions CONCAVITY and ELASTICITY.*

Proof. See the appendix. □

Figure 3: Capital Goods Market: Comparative Statics

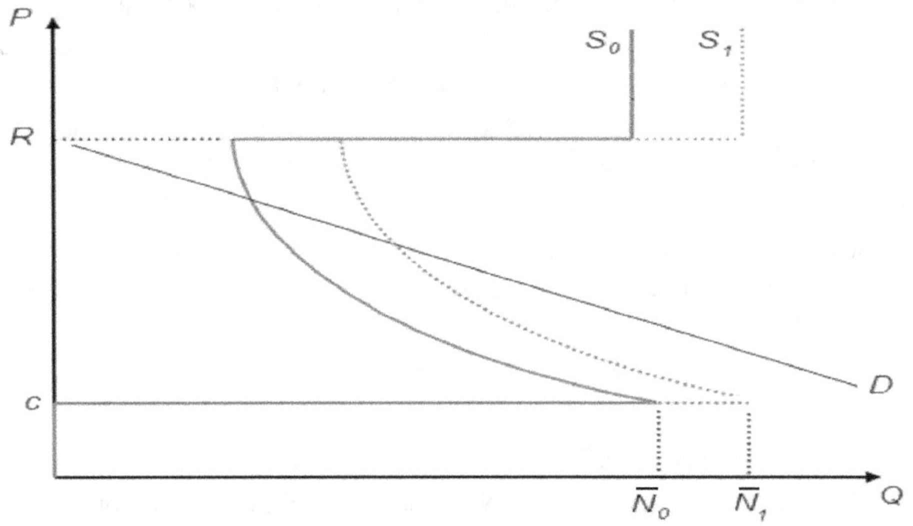

Together lemmas 1 and 2 imply that a higher initial investment in the risky investment in one country creates negative externalities for the other country by making financial crises more severe (i.e., via lower asset prices according to Lemma 1) and more costly (i.e., more fire sales according to Lemma 2).

3.3.3 Banks' Problem

Each bank in country i at $t = 0$ chooses the investment level, n_i, to maximize expected profits given by

$$\max_{0 \leq n_i \leq N_i} \Pi_i(n_i) = q(R-1)n_i + (1-q) \max[R\gamma n_i - n_i, 0] \tag{14}$$

where γ is the equilibrium fraction of rescued assets by a bank in country i which is equal to $1-c/P$ as shown by (9). A bank borrows from the local deposit market at a constant zero interest and invests in the productive asset. With probability q, that both countries are in good times, the investment produces returns as expected Rn_i. Banks make the promised payments to depositors, n_i, leading to a net profit of $(R-1)n_i$. With probability $1-q$, both countries are in the bad state. Banks from the two countries face restructuring costs and hence are forced to fire sale their assets. Since banks are price-takers in the capital market, the fraction of capital that they can save from the fire sales, $\gamma = 1 - c/P$, is exogenous to them. In other words, because each bank is small compared to market size, it does not take into account the effect of its investment choice at $t = 0$ on the equilibrium price (P), and thus on the fraction of assets retained after fire sales in equilibrium (γ).

Banks undoubtedly earn net positive returns in the good state since $q(R-1) > 0$. Moreover, due to the limited liability, they never receive negative profits in the bad state. Because banks do not internalize the effect of their initial investment on the stability of the financial system at $t = 1$, there is no counter-effect that offsets the positive returns on investment. Therefore, a bank's net expected return from risky investment at $t = 0$ is always positive, and a bank always makes itself better off by investing more. Therefore, the regulatory upper limit on the risky investment at $t = 0$ will bind (i.e., banks will choose $n_i = N_i$ at $t = 0$).

Fire sales will be severe for some parameters and banks may become insolvent in equilibrium, as analyzed in Section 5. I assume that when banks are insolvent after fire sales they are required by law to manage remaining assets until the last period and to transfer asset returns into the deposit insurance fund. This is a reasonable assumption because banks are the only sophisticated agents in our model domestic economy that can manage those assets. Furthermore, in practice, the dissolution process of insolvent banks usually does not happen immediately. It is a time-consuming process because, for example, loans have to be called-off or sold to third parties to make payments to debtors. This assumption also captures this time dimension of the dissolution process.

3.3.4 Regulators' Problem

Regulators of the two countries simultaneously determine the regulatory standards for the banks in their own jurisdictions before banks make their borrowing and investment decisions at $t = 0$. Regulation in each country $i = A, B$ takes the form of an upper limit, $N_i \geq 0$, on the investment level allowed for domestic banks. Banks in country i have to abide by the regulation by choosing their investment levels as $n_i \leq N_i$. As they set the standards, regulators anticipate that banks will choose initial investment levels that are as high as possible, and incorporate this fact into their decision problem.

The objective of an independent national financial regulator is to maximize the net expected social welfare of its own country. Social welfare is defined as the expected return to the risky investment minus the cost of the initial investment. Therefore, regulator i chooses $N_i \geq 0$, to solve

$$\max_{N_i \geq 0} W_i(N_i, N_j) = \max_{N_i \geq 0} qRN_i + (1-q)R\gamma^*(N_i, N_j)N_i + (e - N_i) \quad (15)$$

while taking the regulatory standard in the other country, N_j, as given. Let $(\widehat{N}_A, \widehat{N}_B)$ denote the Nash Equilibrium of the game between the regulators at $t = 0$ whenever it exists. I assume that the initial endowment of consumers (e) is sufficiently large, and that it is not a binding constraint in equilibrium.

Social welfare given by (15) incorporates the fact that banks investment level, n_i, equals N_i, the regulatory upper limit. With probability q, the good state is realized when banks in country i obtain a total return of RN_i. With probability $1 - q$ both countries land in the bad state. In the bad state, banks perform asset sales as described previously, and manage the remaining assets,

$\gamma^*(N_i, N_j)N_i$ until $t = 2$, to obtain a gross return of R per unit. Therefore the return to the investment in the bad state in country i is $R\gamma^*(N_i, N_j)N_i$. The cost of the initial investment (N_i) is subtracted to obtain net returns to the investment. Each regulator takes into account the effect of both countries' regulatory standards on the price of capital in the bad state. This is why the fraction of assets that banks can keep after the fire sales, $\gamma^*(N_i, N_j) = 1 - c/P^*(N_i, N_j)$, is written as a function of the regulatory standards in the two countries.

The following equation gives the first order conditions of regulator i's problem in (15)

$$\frac{\partial W_i(N_i, N_j)}{\partial N_i} = qR + (1-q)R\left\{\frac{\partial \gamma^*(N_i, N_j)}{\partial N_i}N_i + \gamma^*(N_i, N_j)\right\} - 1 \qquad (16)$$

By rearranging the terms, we can write this first order condition as a sum of the marginal benefit and marginal cost of increasing N_i, the regulatory standard:

$$\frac{\partial W_i(N_i, N_j)}{\partial N_i} = \{qR + (1-q)R\gamma^*(N_i, N_j)\} + \left\{(1-q)R\frac{\partial \gamma^*(N_i, N_j)}{\partial N_i}N_i - 1\right\} \qquad (17)$$

When regulator i increases N_i, there will be more investment in the risky asset. The first curly brackets give the expected gross marginal benefit from increasing N_i: with probability q, the good state is realized and a total return of R is obtained from the additional unit of investment. With probability $1 - q$, the bad state is realized and a total return of $R\gamma^*(N_i, N_j)$ is obtained from the additional investment. In the bad state, the return can be obtained only from a fraction, $\gamma^*(N_i, N_j)$, of the original investment, because another fraction of the investment is sold to global investors.

The second curly brackets in (17) give the expected marginal cost of increasing N_i. Because $\gamma^*(N_i, N_j)$ is decreasing in N_i, as implied by Lemma 2, a smaller fraction of assets will be retained by banks if the bad state is realized for higher initial investment levels. The first term captures this fact: with probability $1 - q$ the bad state is realized, and an additional unit of investment will decrease the fraction of capital that can be retained by banks of country i by $\partial \gamma^*(N_i, N_j)N_i$, causing a total loss of $(\partial \gamma^*(N_i, N_j)/N_i)N_i$. Last, "-1" in the second curly brackets gives the marginal cost of funds required for the risky investment.

3.3.5 An alternative formulation of regulators' objective function

We can alternatively write the regulators' objective function in a way that explicitly shows the returns to the investment and costs of fire sales. Start by substituting $1 - c/P$ for $\gamma^*(\cdot)$ function, using the derivation obtained in (9) to write (15) as

$$W_i(N_i, N_j) = qRN_i + (1-q)R\left\{1 - \frac{c}{P^*(N_i, N_j)}\right\}N_i + (e - N_i)$$

Add and subtract cN_i to the expression above to get

$$W_i(N_i, N_j) = qRN_i + (1-q)R\left\{RN_i - \frac{Rc}{P^*(N_i, N_j)}N_i + cN_i - cNi\right\} + (e - N_i)$$

Last, rearranging the terms inside the curly brackets gives

$$W_i(N_i, N_j) = qRN_i + (1-q)\left\{RN_i - [R - P^*(N_i, N_j)]\frac{cN_i}{P^*(N_i, N_j)} - cN_i\right\} + (e - N_i) \quad (18)$$

Consider this alternative objective function in detail. It is composed of two main terms as in (15): net expected returns in both the good state and the bad state. Because the first term, $q(R-1)N_i$, that gives the net expected return in the good state is clear, I focus on the latter. The first term inside the curly brackets gives the net total return that could be obtained from the investment if there were no fire sales. The second term is the cost of fire sales: $cN_i \backslash P^*(N_i, N_j)$ is the amount of assets sold in fire sales as given by (10), where banks receive $P^* < R$ from these assets instead of R. The last term inside the curly brackets, cN_i, is the total cost of restructuring.

Because the two versions of the regulators' objective function are the same, I will use the first formulation in the rest of the paper for the sake of analytical convenience, even though the alternative formulation could be more intuitive.

3.3.6 Regulatory Standards in the Uncoordinated Equilibrium

Having analyzed the problem of regulators, we can turn to investigating the equilibrium of the game between regulators at $t = 0$ when they act independently. The aims are to show that there exists a unique symmetric equilibrium of this game, and then to perform comparative statics. I start by analyzing the properties of the best response functions of regulators. The following lemma establishes that independent regulators have a unique best response to each regulatory standard choice by the opponent country.

Lemma 3. *Under Assumptions* CONCAVITY, ELASTICITY *and* REGULARITY, *each regulator's best response is unique valued.*

Proof. See the appendix. □

An interesting question in this setup concerns how that unique best response behaves as regulation in the opponent country changes. Suppose that the regulator of country B decides to tighten regulation (i.e., to reduce N_B). How would the regulator of country A optimally react? The next proposition shows that regulator A optimally chooses to relax its regulatory standard (i.e., increase N_A), as regulator B imposes stricter regulations. In other words, the optimal regulatory standards in the two countries are *strategic substitutes*.

Proposition 1. *Under Assumptions CONCAVITY, ELASTICITY and REGULARITY, optimal regulatory standards in the uncoordinated equilibrium are strategic substitutes.*

Proof. See the appendix. □

The intuition for this result is as follows: If regulator B tightens its regulatory standard by reducing the upper limit on the investment level for its banks, there will be less distressed assets at $t = 1$ in the bad state; hence, a higher asset price will be realized. Therefore, fewer assets will be sold in equilibrium as shown by Lemma 2, which means that banks in both countries will be able to retain a higher fraction of their initial investment after fire sales. This retention will increase the marginal return to investment and initially allow regulator A to optimally choose a higher upper limit on the investment level (i.e. relax its regulatory standard).

The next lemma shows that in order to have finite and strictly positive equilibrium investment levels in the two countries, banks' return from investment R should not be too low or too high. The exact condition on R is given by Assumption $RANGE$, which states that $1 + c(1-q) < R \leq 1/q$.

Lemma 4. *The best responses of each regulator satisfy $0 < N_i^* < \infty$ for $i = A, B$ if Assumption RANGE holds, i.e. if $1 + (1-q)c < R \leq 1/q$.*

Proof. See the appendix. □

$1 + (1-q)c$ is the net expected cost of the investment: each unit of investment requires one unit of consumption good initially. With probability $1 - q$ bad times are realized, in which case banks have to incur an extra restructuring cost of c units of consumption goods per unit of investment. If the return on the investment, R, is less then this expected cost, $1 + (1-q)c$, booth countries' social welfare will be higher without any investment at all. Therefore, if $R < 1 + (1-q)c$, then equilibrium investment levels are zero in both countries. But if $R > 1/q$, then the expected return to the investment in the good state alone will be higher than initial cost of investment, which is 1. In this case, even when the entire initial investment is expected to be lost in the bad state, the net expected return to investment will always be positive. For sufficiently high initial endowment levels, this case leads to a corner solution in which social welfare is maximized by having all endowments invested in the risky asset. I also impose $qR \leq 1$ in order to rule out these inconsequential details and focus on the interesting cases.

Now we are ready to examine the existence of a Nash equilibrium in the game between regulators. The nice features of the objective functions of regulators established above help us to show that a Nash equilibrium exists.

Proposition 2. *Under Assumptions CONCAVITY, ELASTICITY, REGULARITY and RANGE, at least one pure strategy Nash Equilibrium exists in the game between two financial regulators at $t = 0$. Moreover there exists at least one symmetric pure strategy NE.*

Proof. See the appendix. □

The next natural question is whether there are multiple equilibria or there is a unique equilibrium. Fortunately, under the previously stated conditions there is a unique symmetric equilibrium of the game between the regulators, as shown by the following proposition.

Proposition 3. *Under Assumptions CONCAVITY, ELASTICITY, REGULARITY and RANGE, there exists a unique symmetric Nash Equilibrium of the game between the regulators at $t = 0$.*

Proof. See the appendix. □

3.3.7 Comparative Statics for the Uncoordinated Equilibrium

What happens to the unique regulatory standards of the uncoordinated equilibrium in the two countries as good state becomes more likely, or if bank's per unit return from investment, R, increases? The next proposition shows that in both cases, regulatory standards in the two countries are relaxed (i.e., regulators increase the upper limit on the risky investment).

Proposition 4. *Regulatory standards in the uncoordinated symmetric equilibrium become more lax as q and R increase.*

Proof. See the appendix. □

This result is quite intuitive because as the good state becomes more likely (i.e., as q increases), regulators will face the cost of fire sales less often and will allow more investment in equilibrium. But as R increases, returns to investment in both good and bad states also increase, making the investment socially more profitable.

I conclude this section by showing that in equilibrium, price of the capital good at $t = 1$ in bad times must be greater than restructuring costs (c). I tentatively assumed this while discussing banks' optimal fire sales decisions at $t = 1$ after they receive bad shocks. Now it is time to prove this claim formally. Under this result, as I have shown, banks optimally restructure all assets in equilibrium. In other words, as previously stated, scrapping of capital never arises in equilibrium.

Lemma 5. *Under Assumptions CONCAVITY, ELASTICITY, REGULARITY and RANGE, the equilibrium price of the capital good at $t = 1$ in bad times satisfies $P^* > c$.*

Proof. See the appendix. □

Lemma 5 holds because if regulators allow the investment level in their country (N_i) to be too high, they know that they will drive down the equilibrium price below the cost of restructuring, in which case banks do not restructure any assets. Therefore, it is never optimal for any of the regulators to allow such high investment levels, independent of the choice of the competing regulator.

3.4 Internationally Coordinated Regulation

Suppose that there is a higher authority, call it the central regulator, that determines optimal regulatory standards in these two countries. In practice, the central regulator could be an international financial institution such as the International Monetary Fund or the Bank for International Settlements, or it could be an institution created by a binding bilateral agreement between the two countries. I assume that, for political reasons, the central regulator must choose the same regulatory standards for both countries. The question that I address in this section is as follows: Suppose that at the beginning of $t = 0$, national regulators can either set regulatory standards independently or simultaneously relinquish their authority to the central regulator. Would they choose the latter?

I define the central regulator's problem as follows: it chooses the regulatory standards in countries A and B, (N_A, N_B), to maximize the sum of expected social welfare of these countries as given below

$$\max_{N_A, N_B \geq 0} GW(N_A, N_B) = \max_{N_A, N_B \geq 0} \sum_{i=A,B; j \neq i} \{q(R-1)N_i + (1-q)[R\gamma^*(N_i, N_j)N_i - N_i]\} \quad (19)$$

In other words, the central regulator maximizes the sum of the objective functions of individual regulators. For symmetric countries, it is natural to assume that each country receives an equal weight in the central regulator's objective function.[18] I denote the internationally optimal common regulatory standards by $(\widetilde{N}, \widetilde{N})$ and compare them to the regulatory standards in the uncoordinated symmetric equilibrium, $(\widehat{N}, \widehat{N})$.

Another way to state the central regulator's problem for symmetric countries involves thinking of the central regulator as choosing the total investment level across the two countries, $N = N_A + N_B$, to maximize their overall welfare. After determining the optimal total investment level $\overline{N}$, it imposes $\widetilde{N}_i = \overline{N}/2$ for $i = A, B$, where

$$\overline{N} = \arg\max_{N \geq 0} \ q(R-1)N + (1-q)[R\widetilde{\gamma}^*(N)N - N] \quad (20)$$

It is easy to see that the two alternative problems for the central regulator given by (19) and (20) are the same due to the countries' symmetry.

Now we can compare the internationally optimal regulatory standards to the standards that arise as a result of strategic interaction between regulators. The following proposition shows that a central regulator will impose tighter regulatory standards (i.e., a lower N) compared to what would have been chosen by independent regulators.

---

[18]Note that the central regulator does not consider the welfare of the global investors. However, the results of the paper are robust to this generalization.

Proposition 5. $\widetilde{N} < \widehat{N}$, *i.e. the central regulator chooses tighter regulatory standards compared to the standards chosen by independent national regulators in the uncoordinated equilibrium.*

Proof. See the appendix. □

Proposition 5 shows that due to the systemic risk caused by asset fire sales, standards chosen by independent national regulators are inefficiently lax compared to regulatory standards that would be chosen by a central regulator. A central regulator maximizes the total welfare in the two countries and hence internalizes the systemic externalities that arise from fire sales. A central regulator takes into account the fact that allowing more investment in the risky asset by relaxing regulatory standards in one country reduces the welfare of the other country due to higher numbers of fire sales during distress times.

3.4.1 Is voluntary cooperation possible?

We see that risky investment levels will be higher in both countries if regulators act strategically. But will countries ever benefit from relinquishing their regulatory authority to a central regulator that imposes tighter standards in both countries? The following proposition shows that symmetric countries always benefit from relinquishing their authority to a central regulator.

Proposition 6. *If the countries are symmetric then both regulators prefer to deliver their authority to a central systemic risk regulator, i.e., $W_i(\widetilde{N}_i, \widetilde{N}_j) \geq W_i(\widehat{N}_i, \widehat{N}_j)$ holds for $i = A, B$.*

Proof. See the appendix. □

When regulators act independently, each allows investment into the risky asset up to the point where the expected marginal benefit from the risky investment is equal to the expected domestic marginal cost of the investment. However, at this level of investment, the marginal total cost across the two countries far exceeds the sum of the marginal benefits. This happens because neither regulator considers the adverse effect of increasing investment level on the welfare of the other country. Yet, the central regulator can choose a total investment level in the risky asset where the total marginal benefit is equal to the total marginal cost, and hence can improve the overall welfare of the two countries. Therefore, it is in the interest of the regulators of symmetric countries to simultaneously surrender their authority to a central regulator.

4 Asymmetric Countries

In the previous section, we saw that regulators of symmetric countries are always better off by relinquishing their authority to a central regulator. Can a similar argument be made for countries that are asymmetric in some dimensions? In other words, if there are differences across countries, would national regulators still benefit from relinquishing their authority to a central regulator?

In this section, I answer this and the following questions that arise when there are asymmetries across countries: How would the asymmetries affect regulation levels in the two countries in equilibrium? How do central regulation levels compare to regulation levels chosen by national regulators independently? Which countries are more likely to accept a common central regulation?

I focus on differences in returns on the risky investment across countries. In particular, I assume that banks in country A are uniformly more productive than banks in country B. In terms of the parameters of the model, this assumption can be stated as $R_A > R_B$.[19]

Furthermore, to simplify the following analysis, I also assume that $F'(0) \leq 1$ in this section.[20] Under this assumption, global investors will purchase capital only if the price of capital falls below one. This assumption also rules out possible multiple equilibria in the capital goods market at $t = 1$ when there are return differences between countries. Note that from global investors' perspectives, the capital goods in the two countries are still identical at $t = 1$.

The next proposition shows that when regulators act independently, the regulator of the high-return country chooses lower regulatory standards (i.e., a higher N) in equilibrium. This result complies with Proposition 4 in the previous section where we have seen that equilibrium investment levels increase in the return to investments given by R.

Proposition 7. *If $R_A > R_B$, then $\widehat{N}_A > \widehat{N}_B$ in the uncoordinated equilibrium.*

Proof. In the appendix. □

Now we can compare common central regulatory standards to uncoordinated regulation levels when there are asymmetries between the countries. The next proposition shows that in order for a common central regulation to be acceptable to both regulators, it must require stricter regulatory standards in both countries compared to the uncoordinated regulatory standards.

Proposition 8. *There exists no central regulation level $N > \min\{\widehat{N}_A, \widehat{N}_B\}$.*

Proof. See the appendix. □

The proof of Proposition 8 makes use of the envelope theorem to show that welfare of a country is decreasing in the investment level of the other country. In order to forego the authority to

---

[19] This assumption is justified when there is segregation between the investment markets of the two countries. There is both a theoretical and a practical reason for making this assumption. From the theoretical perspective, this assumption shuts down the externality channel that operates through the competition between banks from different countries in loan markets and allows me to focus on regulatory spillovers that operate through asset prices during times of distress. The previous literature considered the regulatory spillovers operating through competition in loan and deposit markets, which shows us when cooperation is justified under those extarnalities (e.g., Dell'Ariccia and Marquez (2006)). From a practical point of view, there are well documented return differences across countries and a large body of literature explains those differences based on levels of technology and human capital as well as institutional factors. I just take the return differences across countries as given and examine the desirability of coordination of macro-prudential policies in a world characterized by those structural differences.

[20] This assumption simplifies the analysis by making the demand function of global investors independent of the return differences between the countries.

independently and optimally choose regulatory standards as a response to the regulatory standards chosen by the other country, each regulator must be compensated by a stricter regulatory standard (i.e., a lower N) in the other country. Therefore, any common regulation level above $\widehat{N}_B$, which is the minimum of the two regulation levels given the assumption that $R_A > R_B$, will always be rejected by regulator A.

This discussion implies that if a common regulation level is accepted by the regulator of the high-return country, it will always be accepted by the regulator of the low-return country. This happens because common regulation reduces investment levels in both countries, as shown by Proposition 11. However, it reduces investment levels more in the high-return country compared to the low return country. Therefore, if the regulator of the high-return country is willing to accept a common regulation level, it will necessarily be accepted by the regulator of the low-return country, as shown by the following lemma.

Lemma 6. *For any common regulation level N such that $W_A(N,N) > W_A(\widehat{N}_A, \widehat{N}_B)$ we have $W_B(N,N) > W_B(\widehat{N}_B, \widehat{N}_A)$.*

Proof. See the appendix. □

Lemma 6 allows us to focus on the welfare of country A in search of mutually acceptable common regulatory standards. We may define N^m as the regulatory standard that maximizes the welfare of country A if it is uniformly imposed in both countries. Formally, I define N^m as follows:

Definition 1. $N^m \equiv \arg\max_N W_A(N,N)$

Given this definition, we can write the net maximum benefit from common central regulation to country A as $W_A(N^m, N^m) - W_A(\widehat{N}_A, \widehat{N}_B)$. The next proposition shows that this net maximum benefit decreases as the differences between the countries become larger.

Proposition 9. *Suppose that $F'(0) \leq 1$. Let $s \equiv R_A - R_B > 0$. Then for any R_A, there exists $\widehat{s} \in (0, R_A - 1)$ such that $W_A(N^m, N^m) - W_A(\widehat{N}_A, \widehat{N}_B) \geq 0$ if $s \leq \widehat{s}$, and $W_A(N^m, N^m) - W_A(\widehat{N}_A, \widehat{N}_B) < 0$ otherwise.*

Proof. See the appendix. □

Proposition 9 provides the main result of this section: if the return differences between the two countries are above a threshold, then at least the high-return country will be worse off if a common regulation level is imposed across the two countries, even if the common regulation is chosen such that it maximizes the welfare of the high-return country. Large return differences will imply that such a common regulation level is too strict compared to the regulatory standard that would be chosen by the high-return country in the uncoordinated equilibrium. Therefore, welfare of the high-return country will fall if it decides to accept common regulatory standards in the face of high return differences between countries. In other words, Proposition 9 shows that voluntary cooperation can exist only between sufficiently similar countries. If the differences across countries are sufficiently high, then at least one of them will be worse off by accepting common central regulation.

5 Extensions: Discussion of Assumptions

In this section I examine the robustness of the main results with regard to changes in some of the assumptions in the basic model. I revisit the assumptions of deposit insurance, limited liability for bank owners, and nonexistence of initial equity capital for bank owners, and show that the qualitative results do not change when these assumptions are relaxed.

5.1 Deposit Insurance

With a deposit insurance fund, banks are able to borrow at constant and zero net interest rate from consumers because consumers are guaranteed by the fund that they will always recover their initial investment. If banks do not have sufficient funds to make the promised payments to consumers following a bad state, the deposit insurance fund steps in and pays consumers the deficit between the promised payment and the resources available to a bank.

What happens if there is no deposit insurance? The answer depends on the competitive structure of the deposit market. I consider two polar cases: first, each bank is a local monopoly in the deposit market; and second, there is perfect competition between banks in the deposit market. I begin here with the local monopoly case and discuss the perfect competition case in Section 5.1.1. When each bank is a local monopoly as in the basic model, the interest on deposit contracts will be just enough to induce risk-neutral consumers to deposit their endowments with them. In technical terms, the individual rationality condition for consumers will bind. I restrict attention to deposit contracts that are in the form of simple debt contracts.[21]

A bank in country i will choose the amount to borrow and invest in the risky asset, n_i, and the interest rate on the deposits, r, to maximize the net expected profits:

$$\max_{r, n_i \geq 0} \quad q(R-r)n_i + (1-q)\max\{(1-c/P)Rn_i - rn_i, 0\} \quad (21)$$

subject to

$$qrn_i + (1-q)\min\{R(1-c/P)n_i, rn_i\} \geq n_i \quad (IR) \quad (22)$$

$$n_i \leq N_i \quad (23)$$

---

[21] There are two justifications for this restriction. First, this assumption is realistic: the deposit contracts are in the form of simple debt contracts in practice. Second, debt contracts can be justified by assuming that depositors can observe banks' asset returns only at a cost. According to Townsend (1979), in the case of costly state verification, debt contracts will be optimal.

where $1 - c/P = \gamma$ is the fraction of assets retained by banks at $t = 1$ after fire sales (which, as before, banks take as given). The bank has to satisfy the individual rationality constraint of consumers given by (22): expected return to deposits must be greater than n_i, the initial deposit of a consumer. A consumer will receive a gross return of rn_i in the good state which happens with probability q. In the bad state, which arises with probability $1 - q$, he will obtain the minimum of the promised payment, rn_i, and the returns available to the bank after fire sales $R\gamma n_i$. If $R\gamma n_i < n_i$ the consumer will experience a loss in the bad state.

As before, the bank is also subject to the maximum investment regulation $n_i \leq N_i$. Because the problem of a bank is still linear, it will yield a corner solution as before: there will be either a maximum investment ($n_i = N_i$) or no investment at all ($n_i = 0$). We can examine the choice of the investment level (n_i) and the choice of deposit rate (r) separately. First, consider the choice of optimal r for a given investment level. We can see from the problem of banks above that for a given P there are two cases to consider:

Case 1 $R(1 - c/P) > 1$. In this case, banks have sufficient resources to cover the initial borrowing from depositors even in the bad state. Therefore, they will offer zero net interest to consumers. Banks will set $r = 1$, and the *IR* condition will be satisfied with equality. Because banks make net positive profits in both states of the world, they want to invest as much as possible. Banks will borrow and invest in the risky asset until the regulatory requirement binds ($n_i = N_i$). Given that banks invest as much as possible, regulators will choose the same standards in equilibrium as in the basic model. Therefore, the symmetric equilibrium of Section 3 and its qualitative results will prevail.

Case 2 $R(1 - c/P) < 1$. In this case, returns on the assets retained by banks after fire sales are not sufficient to cover the initial borrowing from depositors because $R(1 - c/P)n_i < n_i$. Banks have to offer positive net interest rate to consumers in the good state to compensate for their losses in the bad state. For the *IR* condition of consumers to be satisfied, r has to be such that

$$r \geq \frac{1 - (1 - q)R(1 - c/P)}{q} \equiv r^* \tag{24}$$

This can be seen by rearranging the *IR* condition (22), and noting that $\min\{R(1 - c/P)n_i, rn_i\} = R(1 - c/P)n_i$ in this case. Banks will offer consumers the lowest r that satisfies (24) to maximize their profits, and hence will set $r = r^*$. I check if there is an equilibrium where banks make maximum investment and regulators choose the same standards as before for such r^*. Suppose that regulators choose their standards assuming that banks will make the maximum allowed investment. We know, from the analysis in Section 3 that in this case there will be unique symmetric equilibrium regulatory standards given by $(\widehat{N}, \widehat{N})$. Banks will indeed make the maximum investment under these regulatory standards if their expected profit is positive. Because in this case banks receive zero returns in the bad state, their expected profit is equal to $q(R - r^*)n_i$, as can be seen from (21). The expected profit is positive if $R > r^*$ when $P = P^*(\widehat{N}, \widehat{N})$. Using the definition of r^* in

(24) this condition can be written as

$$P > \frac{c(1-q)R}{R-1} \qquad (25)$$

Because $\gamma = 1 - c/P$, this condition can be restated as

$$\gamma \frac{c(1-q)R}{R-1} \qquad (26)$$

In order to see that this is indeed the case in the symmetric equilibrium obtained in Section 3 (when $\gamma = \gamma^*(\widehat{N}, \widehat{N})$), rearrange the FOCs of the regulator's problem given by (16) to get

$$\gamma^*(\widehat{N}, \widehat{N}) = \frac{1-qR}{(1-q)R} - \frac{\partial \gamma(\widehat{N}, \widehat{N})}{\partial N_i} N_i > \frac{1-qR}{(1-q)R} \qquad (27)$$

since $\partial \gamma(\widehat{N}, \widehat{N})/\partial N_i < 0$ as shown in the proof of Lemma 3. Therefore, the symmetric equilibrium obtained under the deposit insurance will prevail when this assumption is removed.

5.1.1 No deposit insurance and perfectly competitive deposit markets

Now, instead of assuming that each bank is a local monopoly in the deposit market, I assume that the deposit market is perfectly competitive and analyze the robustness of the results to this change in the environment. If the deposit market is perfectly competitive banks will earn zero profits because consumers will get all of the returns on the risky investment. Each bank in country i will choose the amount of investment in the risky asset (n_i) to maximize the expected utility of a representative depositor:

$$\max_{0 \leq n_i \leq N_i 0} qRn_i + (1-q)R\gamma n_i - n_i \qquad (28)$$

With probability q, the consumers will receive a gross return of Rn_i, and with probability $1-q$, they will receive $(1-c/P)Rn_i$, which is the return on the assets retained by their bank after fire sales. The cost of the initial investment, n_i, is subtracted to obtain net expected return to deposits. For consumers who choose to deposit their endowments with the bank, the net expected return must be greater than zero, and if it is greater than zero, consumers will choose to invest everything they have. Hence, the regulatory requirement, $n_i \leq N_i$ will bind. But if regulators assume that banks will make the maximum investment, we know from Section 3 that there will be a unique set of regulatory standards given by $(\widehat{N}, \widehat{N})$. Last, we have to check whether banks will indeed chose maximum investment if $(N_i, N_j) = (\widehat{N}, \widehat{N})$. Rearranging (28) shows that the expected net utility of a representative depositor will be greater than zero if

$$P > \frac{c(1-q)R}{R-1} \qquad (29)$$

This is the same condition as (25). We know from the analysis above that this condition is satisfied in the symmetric equilibrium of Section 3, i.e. when $P = P^*(\widehat{N}, \widehat{N})$. Therefore, we can conclude that the symmetric equilibrium obtained under the deposit insurance will prevail when this assumption is removed regardless of whether the deposit market is competitive or each bank is a local monopoly in the deposit market.

5.2 Limited Liability

In the basic model, I assumed that banks are protected by limited liability. Limited liability assumption means that bank profits are (weakly) positive in each state of the world. If returns to the assets of a bank fall short of its liabilities, then the bank owners receive zero profits. Banks have always wanted to make unlimited investment in the risky asset under this assumption. Now instead, suppose that bank owners have some wealth or endowment at the last period that can be seized by depositors if the returns on assets are not enough to cover the promised payments to depositors.[22]

When there is no limited liability, a bank in country i chooses $0 \leq n_i \leq N_i$ to maximize the expected profits:

$$\max_{0 \leq n_i \leq N_i 0} qRn_i + (1-q)R(1-c/P)n_i - n_i \qquad (30)$$

where P is the price of capital in the fire sale market in the bad state at $t = 1$. Each bank takes this price as given. This problem is essentially the same as the problem of banks when there is no deposit insurance and the deposit market is perfectly competitive. This can be seen by comparing problems (21) and (30).

The first order condition for the problem of banks is

$$\frac{\partial \pi}{\partial n_i} = qR + (1-q)R(1-c/P) - 1 \qquad (31)$$

The first order condition will be positive if and only if

$$P > \frac{c(1-q)R}{R-1} \equiv \underline{P} \qquad (32)$$

In other words, as long as $P \geq \underline{P}$, banks will still want to make unlimited investment in the risky asset. But if regulators expect banks to set $n_i = N_i$, they will choose the same set of regulatory standards as in the case with limited liability. Note that as long as regulators internalize the losses of bank owners due to fire sales, their objective function will be the same as (15). Therefore, in order to show that equilibrium regulatory standards do not change when the limited liability assumption is removed, we have to check whether the price of capital in the uncoordinated equilibrium satisfies

---

[22] Instead, the negative utility of bank owners in this case can be interpreted as the disutility of legal punishment for bankruptcy.

$P^*(\widehat{N}, \widehat{N}) \geq \underline{P}$. This is again the same condition as (25). The analysis in Section 5.1 showed that this condition indeed holds in equilibrium. Therefore, the symmetric equilibrium and the qualitative results obtained under the limited liability assumption will prevail when we remove this assumption.

5.3 Initial Bank Equity Capital

In the basic model, I also assumed that banks have no initial endowment of their own that they can invest in the risky asset. Because banks raised necessary funds for investment from the deposit market, the liability side of their balance sheets contained only debt and not any equity capital.[23]

In this section, I assume that banks have an initial endowment of E units of consumption good which they have to invest in the risky asset. This equity is costly: the opportunity cost of equity to bank owners, ρ, is greater than one, the cost of insured deposits. These two assumptions are a common way of introducing equity capital to a banking model (see Dell'Ariccia and Marquez (2006), Hellmann et al. (2000), and Repullo (2004) among others). The assumption that the amount of equity capital is fixed captures the fact that it is difficult for banks to raise equity capital at short notice.

When there is bank equity capital, regulation will take the form of a minimum capital ratio requirement. Let $k_i = E/n_i$ be the actual capital ratio of a bank in country i. In this case, regulation will require banks to have $k_i \geq K_i$, where K_i is the capital adequacy requirement in country i.

Given its equity, and the price of capital goods in the bad state of $t = 1$, each bank chooses how much to invest in the risky asset (i.e., n_i as before) to maximize expected profits:

$$\max_{0 \leq n_i \leq N_i 0} q(Rn_i - (n_i - E)) + (1-q)max\{R\gamma n_i - (n_i - E), 0\} - \rho E \tag{33}$$

subject to the capital regulation

$$k_i = \frac{E}{n_i} \geq K_i \tag{34}$$

Note that $n_i - E$ is the amount of funds borrowed from the local deposit market. We can write the capital ratio requirement condition as

$$n_i \leq \frac{E}{K_i} \equiv N_i \tag{35}$$

This analysis shows that there is one-to-one mapping from capital regulations to the form of regulation used in the main text. The banks' problem does not change: they still want to invest in the

---

[23]The term equity capital should not be confused with the capital good. Any initial endowment of bank owners will still be in the form of consumption good. I use the term "equity capital" to refer to bank owners' own endowments that they invest in the bank.

risky asset as much as possible, as long as the net expected return is positive. The minimum capital requirement binds (i.e., banks will choose $n_i = E/K_i$ in an equilibrium with positive investment levels).

Consider the regulators' problem after equity is introduced to the model. Regulators will anticipate that for a given capital ratio requirement, K_i, banks will choose their total investment level such that this requirement binds: $n_i = E/K_i$. Because banks will raise $E/K_i - E = (1-K_i)E/K_i$ units of consumption goods from the local deposit market, we can write regulators' objective function as

$$W_i(K_i, K_j) = q\left[R\frac{E}{K_i} - \frac{E}{K_i}\right] + (1-q)\left[R\widehat{\gamma}\left(\frac{E}{K_i}, \frac{E}{K_j}\right)\frac{E}{K_i} - \frac{E}{K_i}\right] \qquad (36)$$

The function $\widehat{\gamma}(\cdot)$ is the same as the function $\gamma(\cdot)$ except that it is defined over the minimum capital ratios (K_i, K_j), not over the total investment levels. It represents the fraction of initial assets that a bank retains after fire sales. If we define $N_i \equiv E/K_i$ we can express the objective function above as

$$\max_{N_i \geq 0} W_i(N_i, N_j) = \max_{N_i \geq 0} q(R-1)N_i + (1-q)[R\gamma^*(N_i, N_j)N_i - N_i] \qquad (37)$$

This objective function is exactly the same as the regulators' problem in the main text. Therefore, all qualitative results in the main section will carry on when we introduce costly bank equity and redefine regulation as a minimum capital ratio requirement.

Note that when we introduce costly equity, the net expected return on the risky investment must be sufficiently large to cover the opportunity cost of internal bank equity, ρE, for banks. Otherwise, banks will choose not to invest in the risky asset at all. For this reason, the set of parameters where we have strictly positive investment in equilibrium is smaller under costly equity.

6 Systemic Failures in Regulated Economies

In this section I examine systemic failures when the two countries are symmetric. By systemic failures I refer to the fact that all banks in the two countries become insolvent after fire sales. Systemic failures will occur if the asset prices in the crisis state are so low that the returns from investments that could be retained by banks after fire sales are not enough to cover the promised return to depositors, which is simply equal to the initial value of the investment. Systemic failures might occur even in regulated economies. Because countries are symmetric and we assume perfectly correlated shocks across countries, systemic failures, if they occur, will happen in both countries at the same time. We can write the systemic failure condition in equilibrium as

$$R\gamma^*(\widehat{N}, \widehat{N})\widehat{N} < \widehat{N} \qquad (38)$$

where $\widehat{N}$ denotes symmetric equilibrium investment levels. The left hand side is the (expected) return from investments that could be retained by banks after the fire sales, and the right hand side is the promised payments to depositors, which are simply the initial value of the investment.

For the rest of the analysis I will work with a particular functional form for which I can obtain a closed-form solution for equilibrium investment levels. The technology of global investors is given by: $F(y) = R \ln(1+y)$. I solve the model for this particular functional form in Appendix A. Using this closed form solution, we can show that the systemic failure condition given by (38) above is

$$\widehat{N} > \frac{R}{2c}\left(\frac{R-1-c}{R-1}\right) \equiv N^c \qquad (39)$$

where N^c is defined as the critical equilibrium investment level beyond which banks fail in the bad state (i.e., if $\widehat{N} > N^c$ then banks in the two countries become insolvent in the bad state). We have already seen that $\widehat{N}$ is increasing in q. This helps to prove the following result.

Proposition 10. *Let $F(y) = R\ln(1+y)$. If $1 + c < R < \widehat{R}$ then there exists a $\widehat{q} \in (0, 1/R)$ such that for all $q \geq \widehat{q}$ we have that $\widehat{N}(q) \geq N^c$. In other words, for such R, if the probability of the good state is higher than $\widehat{q}$, banks fail in the bad state in the uncoordinated equilibrium. If $R \leq 1 + c$ then banks always fail in the bad state, and if $R \geq \widehat{R}$ then banks never fail in the bad state where*

$$\widehat{R} \equiv \frac{1}{2}\left(2 + c + \sqrt{c}\sqrt{8+c}\right) \qquad (40)$$

Proof. See the appendix. □

By Proposition 4 we have already seen that equilibrium investment level is increasing in q and R. Proposition 10 shows that if R is sufficiently high, then systemic failures do not occur. In order to prove this, I show that the difference $N^c - \widehat{N}$ is monotonically increasing in R, and that this difference is positive for any value of q if R is sufficiently high. Remember that banks fail if $N^c < \widehat{N}$, which means that they will not fail as long as the difference $N^c - \widehat{N}$ is positive. But if R has moderate values, given by $1 + c < R < \widehat{R}$, then banks fail in the bad state only if the probability of good state, q, is sufficiently high. For moderate values of R, a sufficiently high q leads to systemic failures because $\widehat{N}$ is increasing q, whereas N^c is independent of q as can be seen from (39). Hence, for any value of R such that $1 + c < R < \widehat{R}$, there is a sufficiently high q such that the difference $N^c - \widehat{N}$ is negative. Last, if R is sufficiently low, given by $R < 1 + c$, then total return from maintained assets after fire sales is never enough to cover the initial value of the investment, because $1 + c$ is the marginal cost of funds for the investment if the bad state is expected to occur with certainty. In order to prove this, I show that for these low values of R, the difference $N^c - \widehat{N}$ is negative for any value of q. Therefore in this case, systemic failures will surely happen in the bad state.

The region of parameters for which systemic failures occur in the bad state is illustrated in the left panel of Figure 4. The horizontal axis in Figure 4 measures q, the probability of success, from 0 to 1, and the vertical axis measures R, the return to investment, from 1 to 2. Since we assume that $Rq \leq 1$, we should ignore the region where $Rq > 1$ in Figure 4. This region is shaded by grey. The blue region shows the set of R, q pairs for a given c, for which systemic failures occur in the bad state. Technically, in the blue region we have that $\widehat{N} > N^c$. There are two horizontal red lines in the left panel of Figure 4. The lower one shows $R = 1 + c$, and it is clear from the graph that banks fail for any value of q if $R \leq 1 + c$. The higher red line shows $R = \widehat{R}$, and it is again clear from the graph that systemic failures never occur if $R \geq \widehat{R}$. Last, if R is between the two red lines (i.e., if $1 + c < R < \widehat{R}$), then for any such R there exists some $\widehat{q} \in (0, 1/R)$ such that systemic failures occur if $q \geq \widehat{q}$, as claimed in Proposition 10.

Figure 4: Systemic Failures

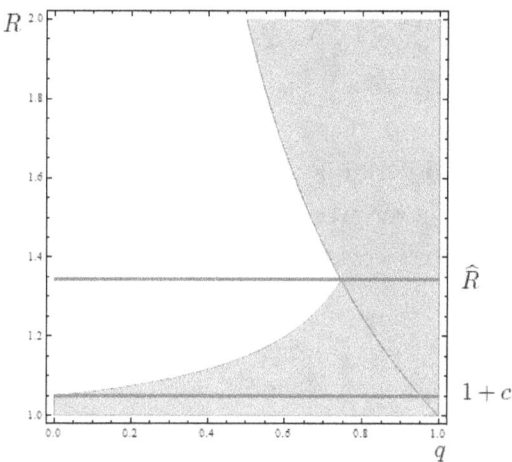 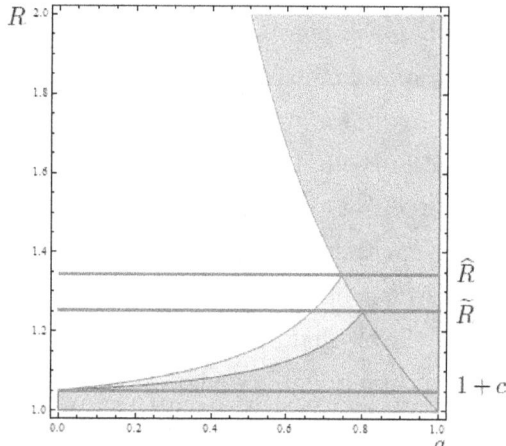

It is clear from the analysis above that systemic failures are more likely when the initial investment level is high. Because central regulation reduces investment levels in both countries, we can claim that moving to a central regulation can eliminate systemic failures. This can be observed from the right panel in Figure 4 where the parameter values for which systemic crisis occurs under the common central regulation are shown in blue. The parameter set for which systemic crisis occurs in the uncoordinated equilibrium is the sum of the colored regions (the same area as in the left panel). It is clear from this right panel that when countries move to common central regulation, the parameter set for which systemic failures occur in the bad state shrinks. The following lemma shows the parameter values under which systemic crisis does occur in the bad state in the uncoordinated equilibrium and moving to a common central regulation eliminates the crisis. Therefore, a common central regulation improves not only the social welfare but also the financial stability of coordinating countries.

Lemma 7. *For any given $R < \widehat{R}$, there exists some $\widetilde{q} > \widehat{q}$, where $\widehat{q}$ is as defined in Proposition 10, such that if $q \in (\widehat{q}, \widetilde{q}]$ moving to a central common regulation from the symmetric uncoordinated* *equilibrium eliminates the systemic failures in the bad state.*

Proof. See the appendix. □

7 Conclusion

I have examined the incentives of national regulators to coordinate regulatory policies in the presence of systemic risk in global financial markets, using a two-country, three-period model. Banks borrow from local deposit markets and invest in risky long-term assets in the initial period. They may face negative shocks in the interim period that force them to sell assets. Asset sales of banks feature the characteristics of a fire sale: assets are sold at a discount, and the higher the number of assets sold, the lower the market price of assets is. The asset market in the interim period is competitive. Each bank treats the asset price as given, and therefore neglects the effects of its sales on other banks. Due to this externality, correlated asset fire sales by banks generate systemic risk across national financial markets.

If the regulatory standard is relaxed in one country, banks in this country invest more in the risky asset in the initial period. If the bad state arises in the interim period, these banks are forced to sell more assets, causing the asset price to fall further. A lower asset price will increase the cost of distress for the banks in the other country as well. Banks may even default in equilibrium if the asset prices fall below a threshold.

I have shown that, in the absence of cooperation, independent regulators choose inefficiently low regulation compared to regulatory standards that would be chosen by a central regulator. A central regulator takes the systemic risk into account and improves welfare in cooperating countries by imposing higher regulatory standards. Therefore, it is incentive compatible for national regulators of symmetric countries to relinquish their authority to a central regulator.

I have also considered the incentives of regulators when there are asymmetries between countries with a focus on the asymmetries in asset returns. In particular, I have assumed that banks in one country are uniformly more productive than the banks in the other country in terms of managing long-term assets. I have shown that cooperation would voluntarily emerge only between sufficiently similar countries. In particular, the regulator in the high-return country chooses lower regulatory standards in equilibrium and is less willing to compromise on stricter regulatory standards.

8 Appendix

8.1 Functional Form Examples

Example 1 $\quad F(y) = R\ln(1+y)$

For this return function we obtain the (inverse) demand function as

$$P = F'(y) = \frac{R}{1+y} \text{ and hence } y = F'^{-1}(P) = \frac{R-P}{P} \equiv D(P) \tag{8.1}$$

This demand function is clearly downward slopping and convex as seen below

$$D'(P) = -\frac{R}{P^2} < 0 \text{ and } D''(P) = \frac{2R}{P^3} > 0$$

$F(\cdot)$ satisfies Assumption $CONCAVITY$ since

$$F''(y) = -\frac{R}{(1+y)^2} < 0 \text{ and since } F'(0) = R$$

Let's check whether this functional form satisfies the conditions given by *Assumption ELASTICITY* and *Assumption REGULARITY*, respectively.

$$F'(y) + yF''(y) = \frac{R}{1+y} - y\frac{R}{(1+y)^2} = \frac{Ra}{(1+y)^2} > 0$$

Clearly *Assumption ELASTICITY* is satisfied. Below we see that this function satisfies *Assumption REGULARITY* as well:

$$F'(y)F'''(y) - 2F''(y)^2 = \frac{R}{(1+y)}\frac{2R}{(1+y)^3} - 2\left(\frac{R}{(1+y)^2}\right)^2 = 0$$

From above we can also see that this return function induces a log-convex demand function since we will have $F'(y)F'''(y) - F''(y)^2 > 0$

Example 2 $\quad F(y) = \sqrt{y + a^2}$

For this example the demand function will be obtained as

$$P = F'(y) = \frac{1}{2\sqrt{y+a^2}} \text{ and hence } y = F'^{-1}(P) = \frac{1}{4P^2} - a^2 \equiv D(P)$$

This demand function is also downward slopping and convex as seen below

$$D'(P) = -\frac{1}{2P^3} < 0 \text{ and } D''(P) = \frac{3}{2P^4} > 0$$

Assumption CONCAVITY is satisfied since

$$F''(y) = -\frac{1}{4(y+a)^{3/2}} < 0 \text{ and } F'(0) = R \text{ implies that } \frac{1}{2a} = R \text{ or } a = \frac{1}{2R}$$

We can easily show that *Assumption ELASTICITY* is satisfied:

$$F'(y) + yF''(y) = \frac{1}{2(y+a)^{\frac{1}{2}}} - y\frac{1}{4(y+a)^{\frac{3}{2}}} = \frac{y+2a}{4(y+a)^{\frac{3}{2}}} > 0$$

Likewise we can show that this function satisfies *Assumption REGULARITY* as well:

$$F'(y)F'''(y) - 2F''(y)^2 = \frac{1}{2(y+a)^{\frac{1}{2}}}\frac{3}{8(y+a)^{\frac{5}{2}}} - 2\left(\frac{1}{4(y+a)^{\frac{3}{2}}}\right)^2$$

$$= \frac{-1}{16(y+a)^3} < 0$$

Note that in contrast to the first example this functional form induces a log-concave demand function since we can show that $F'(y)F'''(y) - F''(y)^2 < 0$

8.2 Symmetric Countries: An example

In this section, I obtain closed form solutions for non-cooperative equilibrium regulation levels and regulation levels under cooperative benchmark for the particular functional form choice for the global investors' technology given by Example 1 above.

For analytical convenience suppose that the technology of global investors is given by the following logarithmic function as investigated by Example 1 above

$$F(y) = A\ln(a+y) \tag{8.2}$$

where the amount of assets the global investors optimally buy satisfies the following first order conditions

$$F'(y) = \frac{A}{a+y} = P \tag{8.3}$$

which will induce a downward slopping demand function

$$y = F'(P)^{-1} = \frac{A - aP}{P} \equiv D(P) \tag{8.4}$$

Imposing *Assumption CONCAVITY* on this functional form gives

$$F'(0) = R \Rightarrow \frac{A}{a} = R \quad \text{or} \quad A = aR \tag{8.5}$$

It is shown in the previous section that this functional form satisfies the conditions given by *Assumptions ELASTICITY and REGULARITY*. Since this functional form satisfies all sufficient conditions, we can proceed with solving for the equilibrium. We start solving the model backwards as in the previous section. Therefore we first find the equilibrium price at $t = 1$ using the market

clearing condition.
$$D(P) = S(P, N_A + N_B) \Rightarrow \frac{A - aP}{P} = \frac{c(N_A + N_B)}{P} \tag{8.6}$$

Hence, we get the equilibrium price of assets at $t = 1$ as

$$P^* = \frac{A - c(N_A + N_B)}{a} \tag{8.7}$$

which is clearly decreasing in the investment levels in both countries. Note also that equilibrium price is determined only by the total investment level in the two countries. Exact division of the total investment between the countries will not affect P^*. This property of the equilibrium price of assets is very helpful in the analysis of the model.

We can also obtain equilibrium fraction of assets retained by banks after fire sales as a function of initial investment levels in each country by plugging the equilibrium price given by equation (8.7) into equation (9) that defines this fraction as a ratio of market price, which will give that

$$\gamma^*(N_A, N_B) = 1 - \frac{c}{P^*(N_A, N_B)} = 1 - \frac{ac}{A - c(N_A + N_B)} \tag{8.8}$$

Remember that regulator i's objective function is

$$\max_{N_i \geq 0} W_i(N_i, N_j) = q(R - 1)N_i + (1 - q)[R\gamma^*(N_i, N_j)N_i - N_i] \tag{8.9}$$

Substituting for $\gamma^*(N_i, N_j)$ from (8.8) gives

$$\max_{N_i \geq 0} W_i(N_i, N_j) = q(R - 1)N_i + (1 - q)\left[R\left(1 - \frac{ac}{A - c(N_i + N_j)}\right)N_i - N_i\right] \tag{8.10}$$

where FOCs can be obtained as

$$\frac{\partial W_i(N_i, N_j)}{\partial N_i} = qR + (1 - q)R\left\{1 - \frac{ac(A - cN_j)}{[A - c(N_i + N_j)]^2}\right\} - 1 = 0 \tag{8.11}$$

Solving for N_i gives the best response function of regulator i

$$N_i^*(N_j) = \frac{A - cN_j - \sqrt{\sigma ac(A - cN_j)}}{c} \tag{8.12}$$

where we define

$$\sigma \equiv \frac{(1 - q)R}{R - 1} \tag{8.13}$$

We can use the best response functions to solve for the symmetric equilibrium investment level.

After some algebra we can obtain that for $i = A, B$

$$\widehat{N}_i = \frac{4A - \sigma ac - \sqrt{8\sigma Aac + (\sigma ac)^2}}{8c} \tag{8.14}$$

Note that by Assumption $CONCAVITY$ we impose that $A = aR$. Substituting for A using this identity gives

$$\widehat{N}_i = \frac{4R - \sigma c - \sqrt{8R\sigma c + (\sigma c)^2}}{8c} \tag{8.15}$$

8.2.1 Central Regulation

Let's consider the central regulator's problem where the central regulator chooses the total investment level in both countries.

$$\max_{N \geq 0} W(N) = q(R-1)N + (1-q)[R\gamma^*(N)N - N] \tag{8.16}$$

Denote the solution to this global problem by $\overline{N}$. Central regulator will impose maximum investment level in each country as $\widetilde{N}_i = \overline{N}/2$ as discussed before. $\overline{N}$ will be characterized by the FOCs of the problem above which we could derive as

$$\frac{\partial W(N)}{\partial N} = qR + (1-q)R\left\{1 - \frac{acA}{(A - c\overline{N})^2}\right\} - 1 = 0 \tag{8.17}$$

Solving for $\overline{N}$ and substituting $\widetilde{N}_i = \overline{N}/2$ gives the globally regulated investment level in each country as

$$\widetilde{N}_i = \frac{A - \sqrt{\sigma Aac}}{2c} \tag{8.18}$$

8.3 Proofs Omitted in the Text

8.3.1 Proofs for the Symmetric Countries Case

Lemma 1. $P^*(n_i, n_j)$ *is decreasing in* n_i *for* $i = A, B$ *under Assumptions* $CONCAVITY$ *and* $ELASTICITY$.

Proof. Applying the IFT on the MC condition gives

$$\frac{dP^*}{dn_i} = -\frac{\partial E(\cdot)/\partial n_i}{\partial E(\cdot)/\partial P} = \frac{\partial S(P^*, n_i, n_j)/\partial n_i}{D'(P^*) - \partial S(P^*, n_i, n_j)/\partial P} \tag{8.19}$$

First, note that using the expression for the total supply function given by (13) we obtain

$$\frac{\partial S(\cdot)}{\partial n_i} = \frac{c}{P} > 0 \tag{8.20}$$

Hence, we can write the derivative in (8.19) as

$$\frac{dP^*}{dn_i} = \frac{c}{P^*D'(P^*) - P^*\left[\partial S(P^*, n_i, n_j)/\partial P\right]} \quad (8.21)$$

The following equivalence will help us to write this derivative using only return function of global investors' return function, $F(\cdot)$, and its derivatives

$$P^*\frac{\partial S(P^*, n_i, n_j)}{\partial P} = P^*\frac{-c(n_i + n_j)}{P^{*2}} = \frac{-c(n_i + n_j)}{P^*} = -S(P^*, n_i, n_j) \quad (8.22)$$

Using this equivalence we can express the derivative given by (8.21) as

$$\frac{dP^*}{dn_i} = \frac{c}{P^*D'(P^*) + S(P^*, n_i, n_j)} \quad (8.23)$$

Let $y^* \equiv S(P^*, n_i, n_j)$ denote the total volume of equilibrium fire sales. In equilibrium we will have $P^* = F'(y^*)$ from the demand curve. Therefore we can obtain

$$D'(P^*) = \frac{1}{F''(y^*)} \quad (8.24)$$

where we make use of the fact that $D'(P) \equiv F'(P)^{-1}$ as given by (3). Hence, we can rewrite the denominator of the expression (8.23) above as

$$P^*D'(P^*) + S(P^*, n_i, n_j) = \frac{F'(y^*)}{F''(y^*)} + y^* \quad (8.25)$$

which we can write equivalently as

$$P^*D'(P^*) + S(P^*, n_i, n_j) = \frac{F'(y^*) + y^*F''(y^*)}{F''(y^*)} < 0 \quad (8.26)$$

This expression is negative since $F''(y) < 0$ by Assumption $CONCAVITY$ and

$$F'(y) + yF''(y) > 0 \quad (8.27)$$

by Assumption $ELASTICITY$. Therefore we conclude that $dP^*/dn_i < 0$. □

Lemma 2. *Equilibrium fraction of assets sold in each country, $1 - \gamma^*(n_i, n_j)$, is increasing in n_i for $i = A, B$ under Assumptions CONCAVITY and ELASTICITY.*

Proof. Using (9) we can write banks' asset sales in equilibrium as

$$1 - \gamma^*(n_i, n_j) = \frac{c}{P^*(n_i, n_j)} \quad (8.28)$$

Note that
$$\frac{\partial \gamma^*}{\partial n_i} = \frac{\partial \gamma^*}{\partial P^*}\frac{dP^*}{dn_i} < 0 \qquad (8.29)$$

since $\delta\gamma/\delta P = c/P^2 > 0$ from (9) and by Lemma 1 we have that $dP^*/dn_i < 0$ for $i = A, B$. Therefore, equilibrium fraction of assets rescued after fire sales (γ^*) is decreasing in n_i for $i = A, B$.

Since equilibrium fraction of assets sold in each country is given by $1 - \gamma^*(n_i, n_j)$, we obtain that this fraction is increasing in n_i for $i = A, B$. $\square$

Lemma 3. *Under Assumptions CONCAVITY, ELASTICITY and REGULARITY, each regulator's best response is unique valued.*

Proof. For this proof I refer to the conditions given by Assumptions $CONCAVITY$, $ELASTICITY$ and $REGULARITY$. I show that if the global investors' return function, $F(\cdot)$ satisfies these conditions, then the objective functions of independent regulators are concave. This also tells us that first order conditions of the regulators problem, which also implicitly defines their best response functions, is monotone and decreasing. Therefore, there is a unique solution to these first order conditions or in other words best response of each regulator is unique valued.

Let's reproduce regulators' objective function here for convenience

$$\max_{N_i \geq 0} W_i(N_i, N_j) = \max_{N_i \geq 0} q(R-1)N_i + (1-q)[R\gamma^*(N_i, N_j)N_i - N_i] \qquad (8.30)$$

FOCs for regulator of country i's problem will be given by

$$\frac{\partial W_i(N_i, N_j)}{\partial N_i} = qR + (1-q)R\left\{\frac{\partial \gamma^*(N_i, N_j)}{\partial N_i}N_i + \gamma^*(N_i, N_j)\right\} - 1 \qquad (8.31)$$

Let's define the following function for convenience

$$v^i(N_i, N_j) \equiv \frac{\partial \gamma^*(N_i, N_j)}{\partial N_i}N_i + \gamma^*(N_i, N_j) \qquad (8.32)$$

Hence, we can write the FOCs simply as

$$\frac{\partial W_i(N_i, N_j)}{\partial N_i} = qR + (1-q)Rv^i(N_i, N_j) - 1 \qquad (8.33)$$

We will show that Under Assumptions $CONCAVITY$, $ELASTICITY$ and $REGULARITY$ we have $v_1^i(N_i, N_j) < 0$, hence the objective function is concave. This also means that the best response functions are unique-valued. Note that in Lemma 1 we have obtained

$$\frac{dP^*}{dN_i} = \frac{c}{P^*D'(P^*) + S(P^*, N_i, N_j)} \qquad (8.34)$$

which is negative as we have shown there. Since $D(P^*) = S(P^*, N_i, N_j)$ by the market clearing condition, we can also express this derivative as

$$\frac{dP^*}{dN_i} = \frac{c}{P^*D'(P^*) + D(P^*)} \tag{8.35}$$

We will use this expression in the derivative of γ^* with respect to N_i below

$$\frac{\partial \gamma^*(N_i, N_j)}{\partial N_i} = \frac{\partial \gamma^*(N_i, N_j)}{\partial P^*} \frac{dP^*}{dN_i} \tag{8.36}$$

$$= \left(\frac{c}{P^*}\right)^2 \frac{1}{D(P^*) + P^*D'(P^*)} < 0$$

Hence we can obtain the second derivative as

$$\frac{\partial^2 \gamma^*(N_i, N_j)}{\partial N_i^2} = -\left(\frac{c}{P^*}\right)^2 G(P^*) \frac{dP^*}{dN_i} \tag{8.37}$$

where we define

$$G(P^*) \equiv \frac{2D(P^*) + 4P^*D'(P^*) + P^{*2}D''(P^*)}{P^*[D(P^*) + P^*D'(P^*)]^2} \tag{8.38}$$

Note that the derivative of $v^i(\cdot)$, which was defined by (8.32), with respect to the first argument is equal to

$$v_1^i(N_i, N_j) \equiv \frac{\partial v^i(N_i, N_j)}{\partial N_i} = \frac{\partial^2 \gamma^*(N_i, N_j)}{\partial N_i^2} N_i + 2 \frac{\partial \gamma^*(N_i, N_j)}{\partial N_i} \tag{8.39}$$

Put the findings above together to get this derivative as

$$v_1^i(\cdot) = -\left(\frac{c}{P^*}\right)^2 \left[G(P^*)N_i - \frac{2}{c}\right] \frac{dP^*}{dN_i} \tag{8.40}$$

again where $G(P^*)$ is as defined by (8.38) above. We will show that $G(P^*)$ is negative under Assumptions $CONCAVITY$, $ELASTICITY$ and $REGULARITY$, and hence $v_1^i(\cdot) < 0$.

Note that using $D(P) \equiv F'(P)^{-1}$ and $P = F'(y)$ we can obtain

$$(i)\ D(P) = y, \quad (ii)\ D'(P) = \frac{1}{F''(y)} \quad \text{and} \quad (iii)\ D''(P) = -\frac{F'''(y)}{F''(y)^3} \tag{8.41}$$

Hence, we can write the expression in the numerator of $G(P^*)$ as

$$2D(P^*) + 4P^*D'(P^*) + P^{*2}D''(P^*) = 2y^* + \frac{4F'(y^*)}{F''(y^*)} - \frac{F'(y^*)^2 F'''(y^*)}{F''(y^*)^3} \tag{8.42}$$

Re-arranging the RHS of (8.42), we obtain

$$\frac{2y^* F''(y^*)^3 + 4F'(y^*)F''(y^*)^2 - F'(y^*)^2 F'''(y^*)}{F''(y^*)^3} \tag{8.43}$$

Note that the denominator of the last expression is negative by *Assumption CONCAVITY*. Rearrange the numerator to write it as

$$2F''(y^*)^2 \underbrace{\left[y^* F''(y^*) + F'(y^*)\right]}_{(+) \text{ by ELASTICITY}} - F'(y^*) \underbrace{\left[F'(y^*) F'''(y^*) - 2F''(y^*)^2\right]}_{(-) \text{ by REGULARITY}} > 0 \qquad (8.44)$$

The expression in (8.44) is positive under Assumption *ELASTICITY* and *REGULARITY* as shown above. This implies that

$$2D(P^*) + 4P^* D'(P^*) + P^{*2} D''(P^*) < 0 \qquad (8.45)$$

i.e. the numerator of $G(P^*)$ which was given by (8.42) is negative. Putting these results together we obtain that $v_1^i(N_i, N_j) < 0$.

The analysis above shows that FOCs of each regulator is monotone and decreasing. Therefore, we conclude that their best response functions are unique valued as desired. □

Proposition 1. *Under Assumptions CONCAVITY, ELASTICITY and REGULARITY, optimal regulatory standards in the two countries are strategic substitutes.*

Proof. Optimal regulatory standards in the two countries are strategic substitutes if and only if the best response functions of regulators are downward slopping. We can apply the Implicit Function Theorem (IFT) on the first order conditions to obtain the sign of the slope of best response functions. This sign is shown to be equal to the sign of the cross derivative of the objective function due to the results in Proposition 1. In order to show that the sign of the cross derivative of the objective function is negative, I again refer to the technical conditions given by Assumptions *CONCAVITY*, *ELASTICITY* and *REGULARITY*. I show that for any (induced) demand function that satisfies Assumptions *CONCAVITY* to *REGULARITY*, this sign is negative and hence optimal investment levels are strategic substitutes.

If N_i and N_j are strategic substitutes we must have $\partial^2 W_i(N_i, N_j)/\partial N_i \partial N_j < 0$. Remember that

$$\frac{\partial W_i(N_i, N_j)}{\partial N_i} = qR + (1-q) R v^i(N_i, N_j) - 1 \qquad (8.46)$$

where

$$v^i(N_i, N_j) \equiv \frac{\partial \gamma^*(N_i, N_j)}{\partial N_i} N_i + \gamma^*(N_i, N_j) \qquad (8.47)$$

hence

$$\frac{\partial^2 W_i(N_i, N_j)}{\partial N_i \partial N_j} = (1-q) R \frac{\partial v^i(N_i, N_j)}{\partial N_j} \qquad (8.48)$$

$$= (1-q) R \left\{ \frac{\partial^2 \gamma^*(N_i, N_j)}{\partial N_i \partial N_j} N_i + \frac{\partial \gamma^*(N_i, N_j)}{\partial N_j} \right\} < 0$$

The sing of equation (8.48) is negative since

(i) $\frac{\partial \gamma^*(N_i, N_j)}{\partial N_j} < 0$ as shown by eq (8.36) and

(ii) for the cross derivative of $\gamma^*(N_i, N_j)$ we know that

$$\frac{\partial^2 \gamma^*(N_i, N_j)}{\partial N_i \partial N_j} = \frac{\partial^2 \gamma^*(N_i, N_j)}{\partial N_i^2} \tag{8.49}$$

since $\gamma^*(N_i, N_j)$ is determined only by the sum of the two investment levels, not by their individual values. Therefore we get an equation similar to the one obtained in the proof of Lemma 3

$$v_2^i(\cdot) \equiv \frac{\partial v^i(N_i, N_j)}{\partial N_j} = -\left(\frac{c}{P^*}\right)^2 \left[G(P^*)N_i - \frac{1}{c}\right]\frac{dP^*}{dN_i} \tag{8.50}$$

which is negative under Assumptions 1 to 3 as shown in the proof of Lemma 3. Hence, the best response functions are downward slopping which implies that N_i and N_j are strategic substitutes. $\square$

Lemma 4. *The best responses of each country satisfy $0 < N_i^* < \infty$ for $i = A, B$ if Assumption RANGE holds, i.e. if $1 + c(1-q) < R \leq 1/q$.*

Proof. **Part 1** If $R \leq 1/q$ then $N_i^* < \infty$.

Let's first define $M = N_A + N_B$ such that

$$P^*(M) = c \tag{8.51}$$

Fix some N_j and consider two exhaustive cases:

Case 1 $N_j < M$.

Define

$$\overline{N}_i = M - N_j \tag{8.52}$$

Consider regulators objective function as $N_i \to \overline{N}_i$

$$\lim_{N_i \to \overline{N}_i} W_i(N_i, N_j) = \lim_{N_i \to \overline{N}_i} q(R-1)N_i + (1-q)[R\gamma^*(N_i, N_j)N_i - N_i] \tag{8.53}$$

Now note that

$$\lim_{N_i \to \overline{N}_i} \gamma^*(N_i, N_j) = \lim_{N_i \to \overline{N}_i} \left(1 - \frac{c}{P^*(N_i, N_j)}\right) = 0 \tag{8.54}$$

since $\lim_{N_i, N_j \to M} P^*(N_i, N_j) = c$ by definition in (8.51). Therefore

$$\lim_{N_i \to \overline{N}_i} W_i(N_i, N_j) = \lim_{N_i \to \overline{N}_i} (qR - 1)N_i \leq 0 \tag{8.55}$$

since $qR \leq 1$ by Assumption *RANGE*. Hence, it is never optimal to choose $N_i^* \geq \overline{N}_i$ in this case.

Case 2 $N_j \geq M$.

By definition of M this implies that $P^*(N_i, N_j) < c$ for any $N_i > 0$. In this case banks optimally discard all capital at $t = 1$, i.e. $\chi^* = 0$ which implies that $\gamma^*(N_i, N_j) = 0$. Hence social welfare in country i will be given by

$$W_i(N_i, N_j) = (qR - 1)N_i \leq 0 \tag{8.56}$$

since $qR \leq 1$ by Assumption *RANGE*. Hence, $N_i^* = 0$ in this case. Therefore we conclude proof of Part 1 by showing that $N_i^* < \infty$ for $i = A, B$ as long as $qR \leq 1$.

Part 2   For the second part of the proof I will show that welfare in country i is always decreasing in N_i when $R < 1 + c(1-q)$, and hence the best responses will be given by $N_i^* = N_j^* = 0$. Remember

$$W_i(N_i, N_j) = q(R-1)N_i + (1-q)[R\gamma^*(N_i, N_j)N_i - N_i] \tag{8.57}$$

Note that the highest value of $\gamma^*(N_i, N_j)$ will be obtained as $N_i, N_j \to 0$. Therefore

$$\text{If } W_i(0,0) < 0 \text{ then } W_i(N_i, N_j) < 0 \text{ for all } N_i, N_j > 0 \tag{8.58}$$

Consider first

$$\lim_{N_i, N_j \to 0} \gamma^*(N_i, N_j) = \lim_{N_i, N_j \to 0} \left(1 - \frac{c}{P^*(N_i, N_j)}\right) = 1 - \frac{c}{R} \tag{8.59}$$

since $\lim_{N_i, N_j \to 0} P^*(N_i, N_j) = R$. Using this we can write

$$\lim_{N_i, N_j \to 0} W_i(N_i, N_j) = \left\{q(R-1) + (1-q)\left[R\left(1 - \frac{c}{R}\right) - 1\right]\right\} N_i \tag{8.60}$$

from which we can obtain $\lim_{N_i, N_j \to 0} W_i(N_i, N_j) < 0$ as long as

$$q(R-1) + (1-q)\left[R\left(1 - \frac{c}{R}\right) - 1\right] < 0 \tag{8.61}$$

Re-arranging this inequality gives

$$qR + (1-q)R + (1-q)c - 1 < 0 \tag{8.62}$$

where further simplification implies $R < 1 + c(1-q)$.

Hence, we conclude that $N_i^*(N_j) = 0$ for $i = A, B$ as long as $R < 1 + c(1-q)$. □

Proposition 2. *Under Assumptions CONCAVITY, ELASTICITY, REGULARITY and RANGE, at least one pure strategy Nash Equilibrium exists in the game between two financial regulators at*

$t = 0$. Moreover there exists at least one symmetric pure strategy NE.

Proof. For this proof, I make use of a theorem due to Debreu (1952) which states that *"Suppose that for each player the strategy space is compact and convex and the payoff function is continuous and quasi-concave with respect to each player's own strategy. Then there exists at least one pure strategy NE in the game."*

I establish below that this game satisfies all three conditions stated in this theorem.

(i) Following Lemma 4 we can restrict strategy space for each regulator to $[0, M]$ which is compact and convex.

(ii) Continuity of the objective function is obvious.

(iii) For concavity we evaluate the second derivative of the objective function with respect to the own action:
$$\frac{\partial^2 W_i(N_i, N_j)}{\partial N_i^2} = (1-q)R\frac{\partial v^i(N_i, N_j)}{\partial N_i} < 0 \tag{8.63}$$
as shown by Lemma 3 above. Hence Nash Equilibria equilibria exist. Existence of a symmetric Nash Equilibrium equilibrium is implied by the symmetry of the game. $\square$

Proposition 3. *Under Assumptions CONCAVITY, ELASTICITY, REGULARITY and RANGE, there exists a unique symmetric NE of the game between the regulators at $t = 0$.*

Proof. I will make use of the theorem that states: *"If the best response mapping is a contraction on the entire strategy space, there is a unique Nash Equilibrium in the game."*

In two-player games best response functions are contraction everywhere if the absolute value of their slopes are less than one everywhere. In order to show this, I make use of the nice feature of equilibrium price function that it is determined only by the sum of the investment levels in the two countries.
$$\left|\frac{\partial N_i^*(N_j)}{\partial N_j}\right| = \left|-\frac{\frac{\partial^2 W_i(N_i, N_j)}{\partial N_i \partial N_j}}{\frac{\partial^2 W_i(N_i, N_j)}{\partial N_i^2}}\right| < 1 \tag{8.64}$$

which can be equivalently stated as
$$\left|\frac{\partial^2 W_i(N_i, N_j)}{\partial N_i \partial N_j}\right| < \left|\frac{\partial^2 W_i(N_i, N_j)}{\partial N_i^2}\right| \tag{8.65}$$

Using the expressions for these derivatives given before this corresponds to
$$\left|\frac{\partial^2 \gamma^*(N_i, N_j)}{\partial N_i \partial N_j}N_i + \frac{\partial \gamma^*(N_i, N_j)}{\partial N_j}\right| < \left|\frac{\partial^2 \gamma^*(N_i, N_j)}{\partial N_i^2}N_i + 2\frac{\partial \gamma^*(N_i, N_j)}{\partial N_i}\right| \tag{8.66}$$

Note that derivative on the right hand side is negative by Lemma 3 and the derivative on the left hand side is negative by Proposition 1. Moreover, $\gamma^*(N_i, N_j)$ and its derivatives are determined only by the sum of the two investment levels, not by their individual values. This implies that

$$\frac{\partial^2 \gamma^*(N_i, N_j)}{\partial N_j \partial N_i} = \frac{\partial^2 \gamma^*(N_i, N_j)}{\partial N_i^2} \text{ and } \frac{\partial \gamma^*(N_i, N_j)}{\partial N_j} = \frac{\partial \gamma^*(N_i, N_j)}{\partial N_i} \qquad (8.67)$$

which implies that $|LHS| < |RHS|$ in (8.66) and hence the slope of best response functions is less than one everywhere on the domain. $\square$

Proposition 4. *Non-cooperative symmetric equilibrium investment levels are increasing in q and R.*

Proof. Using Cramer's rule on FOCs we get

$$\frac{\partial \widehat{N_i}}{\partial \alpha} = -\frac{\frac{\partial^2 W_i}{\partial N_i \partial \alpha} \frac{\partial^2 W_j}{\partial N_j^2} - \frac{\partial^2 W_i}{\partial N_i \partial N_j} \frac{\partial^2 W_j}{\partial N_j \partial \alpha}}{\frac{\partial^2 W_i}{\partial N_i^2} \frac{\partial^2 W_j}{\partial N_j^2} - \frac{\partial^2 W_i}{\partial N_i \partial N_j} \frac{\partial^2 W_j}{\partial N_j \partial N_i}} \qquad (8.68)$$

where $\alpha \in \{q, R, c\}$ is a parameter of the model. First note that

$$\frac{\partial^2 W_i}{\partial N_i^2} < 0, \text{ and } \frac{\partial^2 W_j}{\partial N_j \partial N_i} < 0 \text{ for } i = A, B \qquad (8.69)$$

by Lemma 3 and Proposition 1. Moreover in the proof of Proposition 3 we have shown that

$$\left| \frac{\partial^2 W_i(N_i, N_j)}{\partial N_i \partial N_j} \right| < \left| \frac{\partial^2 W_i(N_i, N_j)}{\partial N_i^2} \right| \qquad (8.70)$$

which implies that the sign of the denominator above is positive. Moreover, in a symmetric equilibrium we will have

$$\frac{\partial^2 W_i}{\partial N_i \partial \alpha} = \frac{\partial^2 W_j}{\partial N_j \partial \alpha} \text{ and } \frac{\partial^2 W_j}{\partial N_j^2} = \frac{\partial^2 W_i}{\partial N_i^2} \qquad (8.71)$$

which allows us to write the derivative as

$$\frac{\partial \widehat{N_i}}{\partial \alpha} = -\frac{\frac{\partial^2 W_i}{\partial N_i \partial \alpha} \overbrace{\left[\frac{\partial^2 W_i}{\partial N_i^2} - \frac{\partial^2 W_i}{\partial N_i \partial N_j} \right]}^{(-)}}{\underbrace{\frac{\partial^2 W_i}{\partial N_i^2} \frac{\partial^2 W_j}{\partial N_j^2} - \frac{\partial^2 W_i}{\partial N_i \partial N_j} \frac{\partial^2 W_j}{\partial N_j \partial N_i}}_{(+)}} \qquad (8.72)$$

the term inside the brackets in the numerator is again negative by the inequality (8.70). Therefore the sing of the derivative above will be equal to the sign of $\partial^2 W_i / \partial N_i \partial \alpha$. To obtain this sign consider the FOCs of regulators' problem

$$\frac{\partial W_i(N_i, N_j)}{\partial N_i} = qR + (1-q)Rv^i(N_i, N_j) - 1 \qquad (8.73)$$

which will imply that in equilibrium

$$v^i(\widehat{N}_i, \widehat{N}_j) = \frac{1-qR}{(1-q)R} \qquad (8.74)$$

Therefore we can obtain that

$$\frac{\partial W_i(N_i, N_j)}{\partial N_i \partial R} = q + (1-q)v^i(N_i, N_j) \qquad (8.75)$$
$$= q + \frac{1-qR}{R} = \frac{1}{R} > 0$$

in equilibrium, using equation (8.33). Hence we conclude that $\partial \widehat{N}_i / \partial R > 0$.

For comparative statics with respect to q consider

$$\frac{\partial W_i(N_i, N_j)}{\partial N_i \partial q} = R - Rv^i(N_i, N_j) \qquad (8.76)$$

which in equilibrium, using equation (8.33) we can write as

$$\frac{\partial W_i(\widehat{N}_i, \widehat{N}_j)}{\partial N_i \partial q} = R\left[1 - \frac{1-qR}{(1-q)R}\right] \qquad (8.77)$$
$$= \frac{R-1}{1-q} > 0 \qquad (8.78)$$

hence we can also conclude that

$$\frac{\partial \widehat{N}_i}{\partial q} > 0 \text{ for } i = A, B$$

i.e. equilibrium investment levels in both countries are increasing as the probability of good state rises. $\square$

Lemma 5. *Under Assumptions CONCAVITY, ELASTICITY, REGULARITY and RANGE, equilibrium price of assets satisfy $P^* > c$.*

Proof. By Proposition 4 we have established that equilibrium investment levels are increasing in both q and R. Since Assumption $RANGE$ restricts $qR \leq 1$, for a given set of other parameters we will obtain the highest investment in equilibrium if $qR = 1$. Consider the FOCs of regulators' problem evaluated at equilibrium regulation standards for $qR = 1$

$$\frac{\partial W_i(N_i, N_j)}{\partial N_i} = qR + (1-q)R\left\{\frac{\partial \gamma^*(\widehat{N}_i, \widehat{N}_j)}{\partial N_i}\widehat{N}_i + \gamma^*(\widehat{N}_i, \widehat{N}_j)\right\} - 1 = 0$$

$$= (R-1)\left\{\frac{\partial \gamma^*(\widehat{N}_i, \widehat{N}_j)}{\partial N_i}\widehat{N}_i + \gamma^*(\widehat{N}_i, \widehat{N}_j)\right\} = 0$$

which implies that

$$\frac{\partial \gamma^*(\widehat{N}_i, \widehat{N}_j)}{\partial N_i}\widehat{N}_i + \gamma^*(\widehat{N}_i, \widehat{N}_j) = 0$$

Lemma 3 has shown that

$$\frac{\partial \gamma^*(N_i, N_j)}{\partial N_i} < 0$$

Therefore for the FOCs above to hold we need

$$\gamma^*(\widehat{N}_i, \widehat{N}_j) = 1 - \frac{c}{P^*(\widehat{N}_i, \widehat{N}_j)} > 0 \tag{8.79}$$

which implies that $P^*(\widehat{N}_i, \widehat{N}_j) > c$ as needed. $\square$

Proposition 5. $\widetilde{N} < \widehat{N}$, *i.e. independent national regulators choose a higher investment in equilibrium compared to the cooperative benchmark.*

Proof. For this proof I use the alternative formulation of central regulator's problem which I reproduce here for convenience

$$\max_{N \geq 0} W(N) = q(R-1)N + (1-q)[R\widetilde{\gamma}^*(N)N - N] \tag{8.80}$$

The FOCs for this problem will be given by

$$\left.\frac{\partial W(\cdot)}{\partial N}\right|_{\overline{N}} = qR + (1-q)R\widetilde{v}(\overline{N}) - 1 = 0 \tag{8.81}$$

where $\overline{N}$ is the optimal total investment level in the two countries. Rearranging the FOCs gives that

$$\widetilde{v}(\overline{N}) \equiv \widetilde{\gamma}^{*\prime}(\overline{N})\overline{N} + \widetilde{\gamma}^*(\overline{N}) = \frac{1 - qR}{(1-q)R} \tag{8.82}$$

where $\widetilde{v}(\cdot)$ is similar to the function $v^i(N_i, N_j)$ except that it is defined over the total investment level in the two countries. The same is true for the function $\widetilde{\gamma}^*(\cdot)$. Now using the fact that globally optimal investment level in each country will satisfy $\widetilde{N} = \overline{N}/2$ we can write

$$\widetilde{v}(\overline{N}) = \widetilde{v}(2\widetilde{N}) = \gamma'(2\widetilde{N})(2\widetilde{N}) + \gamma(2\widetilde{N}) \tag{8.83}$$

Note that equilibrium fraction of rescued assets, $\widetilde{\gamma}^*(\cdot)$, is determined by the sum of the investment levels in the two countries. In other words, exact division of global investment between the two countries do not affect $\widetilde{\gamma}^*(\cdot)$ and hence its derivatives. This property allows us to write $\widetilde{v}(\overline{N})$ as (with a slight abuse of notation)

$$\begin{aligned}\widetilde{v}(\overline{N}) = \widetilde{v}(2\widetilde{N}) &= \widetilde{\gamma}^{*\prime}(2\widetilde{N})(2\widetilde{N}) + \widetilde{\gamma}^*(2\widetilde{N}) \\ &= 2\gamma_1^*(\widetilde{N},\widetilde{N})\widetilde{N} + \gamma^*(\widetilde{N},\widetilde{N}) \\ &= v(\widetilde{N},\widetilde{N}) + \gamma_1^*(\widetilde{N},\widetilde{N})\widetilde{N} \end{aligned} \qquad (8.84)$$

On the other hand, remember that each independent regulator's FOCs will give us

$$\left.\frac{\partial W_i(\cdot)}{\partial N_i}\right|_{(\widehat{N}_i,\widehat{N}_j)} = qR + (1-q)Rv^i(\widehat{N}_i,\widehat{N}_j) - 1 = 0 \qquad (8.85)$$

from which we get that in equilibrium

$$v^i(\widehat{N}_i,\widehat{N}_j) = \frac{1-qR}{(1-q)R} \qquad (8.86)$$

Comparing (8.86) and (8.82) we see that $\widetilde{v}(\overline{N}) = v^i(\widehat{N},\widehat{N})$ where $(\widehat{N},\widehat{N})$ are the symmetric Nash equilibrium investment levels. Using this together with equality (8.84) we can write

$$\begin{aligned}v(\widetilde{N},\widetilde{N}) &= \widetilde{v}(\overline{N}) - \gamma_1(\widetilde{N},\widetilde{N})\widetilde{N} \\ &= v^i(\widehat{N},\widehat{N}) - \gamma_1(\widetilde{N},\widetilde{N})\widetilde{N} \end{aligned} \qquad (8.87)$$

we have previously shown that $\gamma'(N_i,N_j) < 0$ which implies that $v(\widetilde{N},\widetilde{N}) > v(\widehat{N},\widehat{N})$. Lemma 3 has shown that $v^i(N_i,N_j)$ is decreasing in N_i, and Proposition 1 has shown that $v^i(N_i,N_j)$ is decreasing in N_j. Since $v^i(N_i,N_j)$ is decreasing in both arguments, we can conclude that $\widetilde{N} < \widehat{N}$. □

Proposition 6. *If the countries are symmetric then both regulators prefer to deliver their authority to a central systemic risk regulator, i.e. $W_i(\widetilde{N}_i,\widetilde{N}_j) \geq W_i(\widehat{N}_i,\widehat{N}_j)$ holds for $i = A, B$.*

Proof. First, let's define $\widetilde{W_i} \equiv W_i(\widetilde{N}_i,\widetilde{N}_j)$ as the welfare of country $i = A, B$ under central regulation and $\widehat{W_i} \equiv W_i(\widehat{N}_i,\widehat{N}_j)$ as the welfare of country $i = A, B$ under the symmetric non-cooperative equilibrium. Note that by symmetry we have

$$\widetilde{W}_A = \widetilde{W}_B \text{ and } \widehat{W}_A = \widehat{W}_B$$

Since central regulation levels, $(\widetilde{N}_A,\widetilde{N}_B)$, maximize the total welfare of the two countries, $W_A + W_B$, by definition we know that

$$\widetilde{W}_A + \widetilde{W}_B \geq \widehat{W}_A + \widehat{W}_B$$

which implies that $\widetilde{W}_i \geq \widehat{W}_i$ for $i = A, B$. □

8.3.2 Proofs for the Asymmetric Countries Case

Proposition 7. *If $R_A > R_B$, then $\widehat{N}_A > \widehat{N}_B$ in non-cooperative equilibrium.*

Proof. Remember the FOCs of regulator's problem

$$\frac{\partial W_i(N_i, N_j)}{\partial N_i} = qR + (1-q)Rv^i(N_i, N_j) - 1 \tag{8.88}$$

which will imply that in equilibrium we have

$$v^i(N_i, N_j) = \frac{1 - qR_i}{(1-q)R_i} \equiv \beta_i \tag{8.89}$$

Note that β_i is decreasing in R. Since $R_A > R_B$ by assumption, we will have that $\beta_A < \beta_B$. Remember that by $v^i(N_i, N_j)$ is defined as

$$v^i(N_i, N_j) \equiv \frac{\partial \gamma^*(N_i, N_j)}{\partial N_i} N_i + \gamma^*(N_i, N_j) \tag{8.90}$$

$\beta_A < \beta_B$ implies that $v^A(\widehat{N}_A, \widehat{N}_B) < v^B(\widehat{N}_B, \widehat{N}_A)$. Using the expression above this is equivalent to

$$\left.\frac{\partial \gamma^*(N_A, N_B)}{\partial N_A}\right|_{\widehat{N}_A, \widehat{N}_B} \widehat{N}_A + \gamma^*(\widehat{N}_A, \widehat{N}_B) < \left.\frac{\partial \gamma^*(N_B, N_A)}{\partial N_B}\right|_{\widehat{N}_B, \widehat{N}_A} \widehat{N}_B + \gamma^*(\widehat{N}_B, \widehat{N}_A) \tag{8.91}$$

Since $\gamma^*()$, and its derivatives determined only by the sum of the regulation levels, we will have

$$\gamma^*(\widehat{N}_A, \widehat{N}_B) = \gamma^*(\widehat{N}_B, \widehat{N}_A) \tag{8.92}$$

and

$$\left.\frac{\partial \gamma^*(N_A, N_B)}{\partial N_A}\right|_{\widehat{N}_A, \widehat{N}_B} = \left.\frac{\partial \gamma^*(N_B, N_A)}{\partial N_B}\right|_{\widehat{N}_B, \widehat{N}_A} \tag{8.93}$$

Using these two equalities in (8.91) gives

$$\left.\frac{\partial \gamma^*(N_A, N_B)}{\partial N_A}\right|_{\widehat{N}_A, \widehat{N}_B} \left(\widehat{N}_A - \widehat{N}_B\right) < 0 \tag{8.94}$$

From Lemma 3 we know that

$$\left.\frac{\partial \gamma^*(N_A, N_B)}{\partial N_A}\right|_{\widehat{N}_A, \widehat{N}_B} < 0 \tag{8.95}$$

Therefore, for inequality (8.94) to be true we need to have $\widehat{N}_A - \widehat{N}_B > 0$, or equivalently $\widehat{N}_A > \widehat{N}_B$. □

Proposition 8. *There exists no central regulation level $N > \min\{\widehat{N}_A, \widehat{N}_B\}$.*

Proof. By Envelope Theorem we will have that

$$\frac{dW_i(N_i^*(N_j), N_j)}{dN_j} = \left.\frac{\partial W_i(N_i, N_j)}{\partial N_j}\right|_{N_i = N_i^*(N_j)} < 0 \tag{8.96}$$

By assumption we have $\widehat{N}_A > \widehat{N}_B$. Consider a central regulation $N = \widehat{N}_B$. From above we get that $W_B(\widehat{N}_B, \widehat{N}_B) > W_B(\widehat{N}_B, \widehat{N}_A)$. However, by definition $W_A(\widehat{N}_B, \widehat{N}_B) < W_A(\widehat{N}_A, \widehat{N}_B)$, i.e. a central regulation with $N = \widehat{N}_B$ is rejected by Regulator A. Now consider $N > \widehat{N}_B$. By Envelope Theorem we have that

$$W_A(N_A^*(N), N) < W_A(\widehat{N}_A, \widehat{N}_B) \tag{8.97}$$

Moreover, by definition

$$W_A(N, N) < W_A(N_A^*(N), N) \tag{8.98}$$

Hence, any common regulation such that $N > \widehat{N}_B$ will also be rejected by regulator A. $\square$

Lemma 6. *For any common regulation level N such that $W_A(N, N) > W_A(\widehat{N}_A, \widehat{N}_B)$ we have $W_B(N, N) > W_B(\widehat{N}_B, \widehat{N}_A)$.*

Proof. Suppose that $W_A(N, N) > W_A(\widehat{N}_A, \widehat{N}_B)$ for some N. From Proposition 8 we know that such N must satisfy $N < N_B$. Note that we can obtain

$$W_A(\widehat{N}_A, \widehat{N}_B) > W_A(N_A^*(\widehat{N}_A), \widehat{N}_A) > W_A(\widehat{N}_B, \widehat{N}_A) \tag{8.99}$$

where the first inequality is follows from Envelope Theorem given by (8.97), and the second is by definition of optimality. Remember that

$$W_i(N_i, N_j) = qR_iN_i + (1-q)R_i\gamma^*(N_i, N_j)N_i - N_i \tag{8.100}$$

Hence, $W_A(N, N) - W_A(\widehat{N}_B, \widehat{N}_A)$ will be given by

$$qR_A[N - \widehat{N}_B] + (1-q)R_A[\gamma^*(N, N)N - \gamma^*(\widehat{N}_B, \widehat{N}_A)\widehat{N}_B] - [N - \widehat{N}_B] > 0 \tag{8.101}$$

Which we can re-arrange and write as

$$(1 - qR_A)[\widehat{N}_B - N] + (1-q)R_A[\gamma^*(N, N)N - \gamma^*(\widehat{N}_B, \widehat{N}_A)\widehat{N}_B] \tag{8.102}$$

Now consider $W_B(N, N) - W_B(\widehat{N}_B, \widehat{N}_A)$ which will be equal to

$$(1 - qR_B)[\widehat{N}_B - N] + (1-q)R_B[\gamma^*(N, N)N - \gamma^*(\widehat{N}_B, \widehat{N}_A)\widehat{N}_B] \tag{8.103}$$

Now, let's compare (8.102) and (8.103). First note that the first terms are positive in both of them. $\widehat{N}_B - N > 0$ as argued above and it receives a higher weight in (8.103) since $1 - qR_B > 1 - qR_A$ due to our assumption that $R_A > R_B$. Now, if the second terms are also positive, (8.103) will be positive and we are done. However, if second terms are negative, we know that this second term receives a higher weight in (8.102). Hence, if (8.102) is positive in spite of this higher weight on the negative term, (8.103) will necessarily be positive, since it carries a lower weight on the negative term. □

Proposition 9. *Suppose that $F'(0) = 1$. Let $s \equiv R_A - R_B > 0$. Then for any R_A, there exists $\widehat{s} \in (0, R_A - 1)$ such that $W_A(N^m, N^m) - W_A(\widehat{N}_A, \widehat{N}_B) \geq 0$ if $s \leq \widehat{s}$, and $W_A(N^m, N^m) - W_A(\widehat{N}_A, \widehat{N}_B) < 0$ otherwise.*

Proof. Let's see how this difference changes with s

$$\frac{d[W_A(N^m, N^m) - W_A(\widehat{N}_A, \widehat{N}_B)]}{ds} \tag{8.104}$$

this derivative will be given by

$$W_{A1}\frac{\partial N^m}{\partial s} + W_{A2}\frac{\partial N^m}{\partial s} + \left.\frac{\partial W_A}{\partial s}\right|_{N^m, N^m} - W_{A1}\frac{d\widehat{N}_A}{ds} - W_{A2}\frac{d\widehat{N}_B}{ds} - \left.\frac{\partial W_A}{\partial s}\right|_{\widehat{N}_A, \widehat{N}_B} \tag{8.105}$$

Applying envelope theorem reduces this to

$$\left.\frac{\partial W_A}{\partial s}\right|_{N^m, N^m} - W_{A2}\frac{d\widehat{N}_B}{ds} - \left.\frac{\partial W_A}{\partial s}\right|_{\widehat{N}_A, \widehat{N}_B} \tag{8.106}$$

Now note that since

$$W_A(N_A, N_B) = q(R_A - 1)N_A + (1 - q)[R_A\gamma^*(N_A, N_B)N_A - N_A] \tag{8.107}$$

we will have that

$$\left.\frac{\partial W_A}{\partial s}\right|_{N^m, N^m} = 0 \text{ and } \left.\frac{\partial W_A}{\partial s}\right|_{\widehat{N}_A, \widehat{N}_B} = 0 \tag{8.108}$$

Therefore

$$\frac{d[W_A(N^m, N^m) - W_A(\widehat{N}_A, \widehat{N}_B)]}{ds} = -W_{A2}\frac{d\widehat{N}_B}{ds} \tag{8.109}$$

First note that

$$W_{A2} \equiv \frac{\partial W_A(N, N)}{\partial N_B} = (1 - q)R\frac{\partial \gamma^*(N_A, N_B)}{\partial N_B}N_A < 0 \tag{8.110}$$

Moreover, by Proposition 4 we have shown that $\widehat{N}_i$ is decreasing in R for $i = A, B$. This will imply that as s increases (or R_2 decreases), regulator 2 will choose a lower $\widehat{N}_B$ in equilibrium, i.e.

$d\widehat{N}_B/ds < 0$. Therefore,

$$\frac{d[W_A(N^m, N^m) - W_A(\widehat{N}_A, \widehat{N}_B)]}{ds} = -W_{A2}\frac{d\widehat{N}_B}{ds} < 0 \tag{8.111}$$

Hence, the benefit from cooperating is decreasing in the difference between the two countries. Therefore if $W_A(N^m, N^m) - W_A(\widehat{N}_A, \widehat{N}_B) = 0$ for some $\widehat{s}$ it will be negative for $s \geq \widehat{s}$.

We will show that such an $\widehat{s}$ exists. It is clear that for $s = 0$ we have $W_A(N^m, N^m) - W_A(\widehat{N}_A, \widehat{N}_B) > 0$. On the other hand, as $R_B \to 1 + c(1-q)$, we can argue that $\widehat{N}_B$ will necessarily become zero. From Proposition 11 we know that for central regulation be acceptable by regulator 1, we must have $N^m < \widehat{N}_B$. However, as $\widehat{N}_B \to 0$, it won't be possible to reduce $\widehat{N}_B$ sufficiently to compensate regulator 1. Therefore, we will have $W_A(N^m, N^m) - W_A(\widehat{N}_A, \widehat{N}_B) < 0$ for sufficiently large s. By continuity an $\widehat{s}$ such that $W_A(N^m, N^m) - W_A(\widehat{N}_A, \widehat{N}_B) = 0$ must exist. □

8.3.3 Proof of the Systemic Failure Exercise

Proposition 10. *Let $F(y) = R\ln(1+y)$. If $1 + c < R < \widehat{R}$ then there exists a $\widehat{q} \in (0, 1/R)$ such that for all $q \geq \widehat{q}$ we have that $\widehat{N}(q) \geq N^c$. In other words, if the probability of the good state is higher than $\widehat{q}$, banks fail in the bad state in non-competitive equilibrium. If $R \leq 1 + c$ then banks always fail in the bad state, and if $R \geq \widehat{R}$ then banks never fail in the bad state where $\widehat{R}$ is given by*

$$\widehat{R} \equiv \frac{1}{2}\left(2 + c + \sqrt{c}\sqrt{8+c}\right) \tag{8.112}$$

Proof. By Proposition 4 we have already shown that equilibrium investment level is increasing in q and R. Fix some R. Note that, if $\widehat{N}(R, 1/R, c) < N^c$, then $\widehat{N}(R, q, c) < \widehat{N}^c$ for all $q \in [0, 1/R]$ since $\widehat{N}$ is increasing in q.

I will first show that when $q = 1/R$, the difference $N^c - \widehat{N}$ is monotonically increasing in R. Moreover, it is negative when R is small and positive for sufficiently high R. Therefore, we will establish using Intermediate Value Theorem that there exists some $\widehat{R}$ such that $N^c(\widehat{R}, c) - \widehat{N}(\widehat{R}, 1/\widehat{R}, c) = 0$. Using definitions of N^c and $\widehat{N}$ we can write this difference as

$$N^c - \widehat{N} = \frac{aR}{2c}\left(\frac{R - 1 - c}{R - 1}\right) - \frac{a\left(4R - c\sigma - \sqrt{8c\sigma R + (c\sigma)^2}\right)}{8c} \tag{8.113}$$

where

$$\sigma = \frac{(1-q)R}{R-1}$$

as defined before. Evaluating this difference at $q = 1/R$ gives that

$$N^c - \widehat{N} = \frac{aR}{2c}\left(\frac{R-1-c}{R-1}\right) - \frac{a\left(4R - c - \sqrt{8cR + c^2}\right)}{8c} \tag{8.114}$$

We can determine the behavior of this difference as R changes by looking at the derivative with respect to R which will be given by

$$\frac{\partial \left(N^c - \widehat{N}\right)}{\partial R} = \frac{aR}{2c}\left(\frac{(R-1)^2 + c}{(R-1)^2} - 1 + \frac{\sqrt{8cR+c^2}}{c}\right) > 0 \qquad (8.115)$$

This derivative is clearly positive, which means that the difference is monotonically increasing in R. Moreover, note that given $q = 1/R$

$$\lim_{R \to 1+c} \left\{N^c(R,c) - \widehat{N}(R,q,c)\right\} < 0 \qquad (8.116)$$

This follows since $N^c(R,c) \to 0$ as $R \to 1+c$, which can be clearly seen from the definition of $N^c(R,c)$. We know that $\widehat{N}(R,q,c) > 0$ as $R \to 1+c$ since by Proposition 3 we have established that equilibrium investment levels are positive as long as $R > 1 + c(1-q)$. To complete the argument, I will show that when $q = 1/R$

$$\lim_{R \to \infty} \left\{N^c(R,c) - \widehat{N}(R,q,c)\right\} > 0 \qquad (8.117)$$

In order to see this we can expand the difference $N^c - \widehat{N}$ given by (8.114) to write it as

$$N^c - \widehat{N} = \frac{aR}{2c}\left(\frac{-c}{R-1} - \frac{c}{4} + \frac{\sqrt{8cR+c^2}}{4}\right) \qquad (8.118)$$

Now, note that as R becomes large the first term inside the parenthesis goes to zero whereas the last term goes to infinity. Therefore this difference is definitely positive for large R. Now, using the Intermediate Value Theorem we can conclude that there exists some $\widehat{R} > 1 + c$ such that $\widehat{N}(\widehat{R}, 1/\widehat{R}, c) = N^c(\widehat{R}, c)$. Using the definitions of $\widehat{N}$, and N^c from equations (39) and (39) respectively we can solve for $\widehat{R}$ as follows

$$\widehat{R} = \frac{1}{2}\left(2 + c + \sqrt{c}\sqrt{8+c}\right) \qquad (8.119)$$

Case 1 $\quad R \geq \widehat{R}$

The analysis above implies that for $R \geq \widehat{R}$ we have that $\widehat{N}(R, 1/R, c) \leq N^c(R, c)$. Moreover, since for any given R, the highest value of $\widehat{N}$ is obtained when $q = 1/R$, we will also have that for $R \geq \widehat{R}$ we have $\widehat{N}(R, q, c) \leq N^c(R, c)$ for all $q \in [0, 1/R]$. In other words, if $R \geq \widehat{R}$, banks never fail in the bad state for any value of $q \in [0, 1/R]$.

Case 2 $\quad 1 + c < R < \widehat{R}$.

In this case we can show that

$$\lim_{q\to 0}\widehat{N}(R,q,c) < N^c < \lim_{q\to 1/R}\widehat{N}(R,q,c) \qquad (8.120)$$

Hence by the Intermediate Value Theorem we will conclude that there exists $\widehat{q} \in (0, 1/R)$ such that $\widehat{N}(\widehat{q}) = N^c$. Therefore, banks will fail in the bad state if $q \geq \widehat{q}$, and they will survive otherwise. First, I will consider the first part of the inequality in (8.120). It will be useful to note that

$$\lim_{q\to 0}\sigma = \frac{R}{R-1} \quad \text{and} \quad \lim_{q\to 1/R}\sigma = 1 \qquad (8.121)$$

Therefore let's consider $\widehat{N}$ when $q = 0$ and check whether it is less than N^c

$$\frac{a\left(4R - \frac{cR}{R-1} - \sqrt{8Rc\frac{R}{R-1} + \left(\frac{R}{R-1}\right)^2}\right)}{8c} <^? \frac{aR}{2c}\left(\frac{R-1-c}{R-1}\right) \qquad (8.122)$$

where left hand side of the inequality is $\widehat{N}$ evaluated when $q = 0$, and right hand side is N^c given by (39). Simplifying both sides reduces this comparison to

$$4aR - \frac{acR}{R-1} - a\sqrt{8Rc\frac{R}{R-1} + \left(\frac{R}{R-1}\right)^2} <^? 4aR - \frac{4acR}{R-1} \qquad (8.123)$$

simplifying further yields

$$\frac{c}{R-1} <^? 1 \qquad (8.124)$$

which is true as long as $1 + c < R$ as we proposed for this case.

For the second part of the inequality (8.120) consider $\widehat{N}$ when $q = 1/R$ and check when it is greater than N^c

$$\frac{a\left(4R - c - \sqrt{8Rc + c^2}\right)}{8c} >^? \frac{aR}{2c}\left(\frac{R-1-c}{R-1}\right) \qquad (8.125)$$

where the left hand side of the inequality is $\widehat{N}$ evaluated when $q = 1/R$, and right hand side is N^c given by (39). Simplifying reduces this comparison to

$$4aR - ac - a\sqrt{8Rc + c^2} >^? 4aR - \frac{4acR}{R-1} \qquad (8.126)$$

Solving for R yields that this inequality is true as long as

$$R < \frac{1}{2}\left(2 + c + \sqrt{c}\sqrt{8+c}\right) \equiv \widehat{R} \qquad (8.127)$$

Therefore we can conclude that if $1 + c < R < \widehat{R}$, there exists $\widehat{q} \in (0, 1/R)$ such that $\widehat{N}(q) > N^c$ for $q \geq \widehat{q}$. In words, when $1 + c < R < \widehat{R}$ banks fail systemically in the bad state if $q \geq \widehat{q}(R)$, and they survive if $q < \widehat{q}(R)$.

Case 3 $1 + c(1 - q) < R \leq 1 + c$

We know that when $1 + c(1 - q) < R \leq 1 + c$ we will have $N^c(R, c) = 0$ by definition and $\widehat{N}(R, q, c) > 0$ from Proposition 3. Therefore, we will have that $\widehat{N}(R, q, c) \geq N^c$ whenever $1 + c(1 - q) < R \leq 1 + c$ for all $q \in [0, 1/R]$. Therefore banks always fail in the bad state in this case.   □

Lemma 7. *For any given $R < \widehat{R}$, there exists some $\widetilde{q} > \widehat{q}$, where $\widehat{q}$ is as defined in Proposition 10, such that if $q \in (\widehat{q}, \widetilde{q}]$ moving to a central common regulation from the symmetric uncoordinated equilibrium will eliminate the systemic failure in the bad state.*

Proof. We know that systemic crises happen when initial investment levels are high. If initial investment levels are close to the critical borders beyond which systemic crises occur, i.e. $\widehat{N}(\cdot)$ is slightly above $N^c(\cdot)$, then moving to global regulation can reduce investment levels in both countries to $\widetilde{N} < N^c$, and eliminate systemic failures in the bad state.

We can follow the similar lines in the proof of Proposition 10, and show that if $1 + c < R < \widetilde{R}$ then there exists a $\widetilde{q} \in (0, 1/R)$ such that for all $q \geq \widetilde{q}$ we have that $\widetilde{N}(q) \geq N^c$. In other words, for such R, if the probability of the good state is higher than $\widetilde{q}$, banks fail in the bad state under common central regulation. If $R \leq 1 + c$ then banks always fail in the bad state, and if $R \geq \widetilde{R}$ then banks never fail in the bad state where

$$\widetilde{R} \equiv \frac{1}{2}\left(2 + c + \sqrt{c}\sqrt{4 + c}\right) \tag{8.128}$$

It is clear that $\widetilde{R} < \widehat{R} \equiv (1/2)\left(2 + c + \sqrt{c}\sqrt{8 + c}\right)$. We can also show that $1/R > \widetilde{q} > \widehat{q}$ which will complete the proof.   □

References

Acharya, V. (2003). Is the international convergence of capital adequacy regulation desirable? *The Journal of Finance 58*(6), 2745–2782.

Acharya, V. (2009). A theory of systemic risk and design of prudential bank regulation. *Journal of Financial Stability 5*(3), 224–255.

Acharya, V., H. Shin, and T. Yorulmazer (2010). Fire-sale fdi.

Acharya, V. and T. Yorulmazer (2008). Cash-in-the-market pricing and optimal resolution of bank failures. *Review of Financial Studies 21*(6), 2705–2742.

Aguiar, M. and G. Gopinath (2005). Fire-sale foreign direct investment and liquidity crises. *Review of Economics and Statistics 87*(3), 439–452.

Allen, F. and D. Gale (1994). Limited market participation and volatility of asset prices. *The American Economic Review*, 933–955.

Allen, F. and D. Gale (1998). Optimal financial crises. *The Journal of Finance 53*(4), 1245–1284.

Amir, R. (1996). Cournot oligopoly and the theory of supermodular games. *Games and Economic Behavior 15*(2), 132–148.

Barth, J., G. Caprio, and R. Levine (2008). Bank regulations are changing: For better or worse? *Comparative Economic Studies 50*(4), 537–563.

Basel (1988). International convergence of capital measurement and capital standards. *Bank for International Settlements*.

Bengui, J. (2011). Macro-prudential policy coordination and global regulatory spillovers. *University of Maryland, Manuscript*.

Cooper, R. (1985). Economic interdependence and coordination of economic policies. *Handbook of international economics 2*, 1195–1234.

Coval, J. and E. Stafford (2007). Asset fire sales (and purchases) in equity markets. *Journal of Financial Economics 86*(2), 479–512.

Dalen, D. and T. Olsen (2003). Regulatory competition and multinational banking. *CESifo Working Paper Series*.

Dell'Ariccia, G. and R. Marquez (2006). Competition among regulators and credit market integration. *Journal of Financial Economics 79*(2), 401–430.

Gai, P., S. Kapadia, S. Millard, and A. Perez (2008). Financial innovation, macroeconomic stability and systemic crises. *The Economic Journal 118*(527), 401–426.

Hamada, K. (1974). Alternative exchange rate systems and the interdependence of monetary policies. *National Monetary Policies and the International Financial System, University of Chicago Press, Chicago*, 13–33.

Hamada, K. (1976). A strategic analysis of monetary interdependence. *The Journal of Political Economy*, 677–700.

Hellmann, T., K. Murdock, and J. Stiglitz (2000). Liberalization, moral hazard in banking, and prudential regulation: Are capital requirements enough? *American Economic Review*, 147–165.

Holthausen, C. and T. Rønde (2004). Cooperation in international banking supervision. *Working Paper Series*.

Kiyotaki, N. and J. Moore (1997). Credit cycles. *The Journal of Political Economy 105*(2), 211–248.

Korinek, A. (2011). Systemic risk-taking: amplification effects, externalities, and regulatory responses. *ECB Working Paper No. 1345*.

Krugman, P. (2000). Fire-sale fdi. In *Capital flows and the emerging economies: theory, evidence, and controversies*, pp. 43–60. University of Chicago Press.

Lorenzoni, G. (2008). Inefficient credit booms. *The Review of Economic Studies 75*(3), 809–833.

Persson, T. and G. Tabellini (1995). Double-edged incentives: Institutions and policy coordination. *Handbook of international economics 3*, 1973–2030.

Pulvino, T. (2002). Do asset fire sales exist? an empirical investigation of commercial aircraft transactions. *The Journal of Finance 53*(3), 939–978.

Repullo, R. (2004). Capital requirements, market power, and risk-taking in banking. *Journal of financial Intermediation 13*(2), 156–182.

Shleifer, A. and R. Vishny (1992). Liquidation values and debt capacity: A market equilibrium approach. *The Journal of Finance*, 1343–1366.

Townsend, R. (1979). Optimal contracts and competitive markets with costly state verification. *Journal of Economic theory 21*(2), 265–93.

Williamson, O. (1988). Corporate finance and corporate governance. *The Journal of Finance*, 567–591.

www.ingramcontent.com/pod-product-compliance
Lightning Source LLC
Chambersburg PA
CBHW081859170526
45167CB00007B/3072